CHEAP
SLEEPS
in ITALY

**A Guide to More Than 100
Charming, Comfortable,
and Inexpensive Hotels and
Pensiones in Florence,
Rome, and Venice**

SANDRA A. GUSTAFSON

CHRONICLE BOOKS

SAN FRANCISCO

FOR JOAN

Printed in the United States of America.

Library of Congress Cataloging-in-Publication Data
Gustafson, Sandra A.
    Cheap sleeps in Italy : a guide to more than 100 charming, comfortable, and inexpensive hotels and pensiones in Florence, Rome, and Venice / Sandra A. Gustafson
        p. cm.
    Includes index.
    ISBN 0-8118-0234-5 (pbk.)
    1. Hotels, taverns, etc.—Italy—Rome—Guidebooks. 2. Hotels, taverns, etc.—Italy—Venice—Guidebooks. 3. Hotels, taverns, etc.—Italy—Florence—Guidebooks. 4. Tourist camps, hostels, etc.—Italy—Rome—Guidebooks. 5. Tourist camps, hostels, etc.—Italy—Venice—Guidebooks. 6. Tourist camps, hostels, etc.—Italy—Florence—Guidebooks. I. Title.
    TX907.5.I82R664 1993
    647.944501—dc   92-34854
                                                             CIP

Editing: Carolyn Miller
Cover design: Robin Weiss
Cover photograph: Andrew Jasvewski
Cover map: Historic Urban Plans, Ithaca, N.Y.
Book design: Words & Deeds

Distributed in Canada by
Raincoast Books
112 East Third Avenue
Vancouver, B.C. V5T 1C8

10 9 8 7 6 5 4 3 2 1

Chronicle Books
275 Fifth Street
San Francisco, California 94103

Wilcox

CONTENTS

To the Reader

I realize that every day my heart is Italian.

— Stendhal

Italy has played host to visitors for more than 2,000 years. Despite tangled red tape, long lines, and the Italian fascination with complicating a simple issue, if you develop a sense of *pazienza* (patience) you will survive well. With a healthy dose of this *pazienza* and *Cheap Sleeps in Italy* in tow, your trip to Italy will be nothing short of wonderful.

Cheap Sleeps in Italy is not for those travelers who are looking for the cheapest places to stay in Florence, Rome, and Venice. Rather it is for those who are concerned with having a better trip by saving money and not sacrificing comfort in the bargain. As noted travel authority Arthur Frommer says, "The difference between a luxury hotel and a budget hotel is purely one of psychology. When you are in bed at night and close your eyes, what is really important is that the bed is a decent bed and the mattress is relatively firm." I would add that the room should be clean, the bathroom spotless, and the attitude of the management welcoming.

When the dollar was strong, the hotel situation in Italy was easy. If you wanted luxury and total comfort, you paid for it. If you wanted a simple pensione with charm, character, and a low rate, you could find it easily. Or, if you wanted only a clean place to spend the night, you could find that too. Things have changed, and not for the better from a budget point of view. Remodeling and redecorating have come to the hotel industry. What used to be cheap and charming is now more expensive and modern, with extras such as mini-bars, hair dryers, and color TVs. These do not really add anything to your trip, but they do justify management doubling or tripling the rates. The result is that what was once an affordable family hotel or pensione with character and a view, now costs more than $175 per night—without breakfast. As for breakfast, this is a real money-maker for the hotel and a budget-killer for you. If the strong coffee does not wake you, the high cost of the hotel breakfast will. Convenience is the reason why so many eat at the hotel, but the cost is usually outrageous, from 7,000 to 8,000 lire per person to as much as 25,000! In the bottom of the budget category, the truly Cheap Sleep is also gone, but the really bad news is that these budget hotels still have marginal service, no lifts, garage-sale furnishings, and plumbing installed pre-Caesar, or so it seems, and rates that have kept perfect pace with spiraling Italian inflation. Despite all of these gloomy realities, it is still possible to find a comfortable room that is reasonably priced, and of course, *Cheap Sleeps in Italy* will show you how.

The hotel price you pay can depend largely on when you go. A room that costs over $200 in the high seasons may be as much as 50 percent less in the low seasons. The low seasons are generally in August and from December through March. They can extend anytime business is slow, so it always pays to ask for a lower rate, no matter when you are reserving your room. If you do travel in the high seasons, alternatives to the $200-per-night room do exist, but you may find yourself in a religious dormitory or carrying your own luggage up several flights of stairs, doing without air-conditioning, and looking for the shower down the hall.

The way smaller hotels hold down prices is by keeping the decor simple, limiting services, and otherwise running a no-frills operation. This may translate to Formica furniture, linoleum floors, fewer pictures on the walls, skimpy curtains, and little closet space. Almost invariably it will mean the absence of a shower curtain, even in some three-star hotels. The concept of the shower curtain has not yet been embraced by hoteliers in Italy. "The water eventually evaporates," is what they tell you when you ask why this civilized invention is so seldom found.

It is important for readers to know that I do not include any listing, no matter how many raves it has or how many people write to me about it, that I have not personally seen. I assess the facilities, the attitude of the management, and the overall ambience on my unannounced visits. I am on the lookout for dust, mold, mildew, thin towels, scratchy toilet paper, and cigarette burns on the bedspreads. I look for somewhere to put luggage, a place to put a toothbrush in the bathroom, and enough closet space to hold the contents of more than a carry-on flight bag. In the name of research, I have walked countless miles in every type of weather from driving rain to blistering heat, worn out several pairs of shoes, never taken a day off, and loved every minute of it.

Some of the hotels in *Cheap Sleeps in Italy* are cozy, quaint, and rustic, full of charm and personality and with views you will never forget. Others are just right for romantic stays, while a few will be a bit faded around the edges, but with some redeeming virtues. Still others may have been renovated and have the latest word in bathroom plumbing. Some are cheap, others not very, and yet others fall into the Big Splurge category. All have the essential ingredient of giving value for your money.

In addition to offering budget-minded travelers the best advice about hotel values in Florence, Rome, and Venice, *Cheap Sleeps in Italy* provides shopping tips for the smart shopper who feels that no trip is complete without a few hours spent browsing and buying.

To get the most out of any trip, it is important that you know what you want from your trip, which things you can and cannot do without, and the trade-offs you will accept to hold down your costs. Travel with an open mind. When you leave home, do not expect to encounter your way of life again until you return. Enjoy all the new sights, people, and sounds around you. Sample different foods, make an attempt at a few words of the language, and remember that a smile is acceptable in any language. If you can do these things, you will come home a more knowledgeable person, with a lifetime of happy memories.

One of the benefits and joys of my job is discovering hidden treasures and passing them along to you. This edition of *Cheap Sleeps in Italy* is full of wonderful addresses that will make your stay truly special and set the stage for many return visits. At the back of the book is an address where you can write to me and tell me about your experiences. Your comments and suggestions are very important to me, so please take a minute or two and let me know about your trip. In the meantime, I wish you *buon riposo* and, of course, *buon viaggio.*

General Information

TIPS FOR CHEAP SLEEPS IN ITALY

1. Go in an off season when rates are lower and tourists fewer. Be sure the quoted rate includes service and taxes.

2. Make reservations ahead. This not only assures you of a room in a hotel of your choice that is also within your budget, but avoids valuable time spent on arrival in search of a hotel room, rather than relaxing in a *caffè* or enjoying the places you came to see.

3. For first- or second-time visitors, the location of your hotel can make or break your trip. Centrally located hotels are better than someplace listed as "near Rome," or "in the Florence area," that requires long commutes by bus, subway, or taxi.

4. Ask to have the cost of the hotel breakfast deducted from your total bill. In some cases, hotels charge 25,000 lire per person for a breakfast consisting of a roll, coffee, jam, and butter—and, if you are lucky, a glass of canned orange juice. If you multiply this times two or three people for several days, it adds up to a ridiculous amount of money. Instead, do as the Italians do and have a breakfast cappuccino and *cornetto* (roll) standing at the bar at the corner *caffè*. You will save enough to splurge on a great dinner or a special purchase.

5. Inspection of the room before selection is strongly recommended.

6. A room with a double bed (*matrimoniale*) and shower will be cheaper than a twin-bedded room (*due letti*) with a bathtub. Also consider the cost of showers if you are in a room with no facilities. If there are two or three of you, a room with a shower might be just about the same as one without when you add the cost of showers per person per day.

7. If you are a light sleeper, ask for a quiet room, but be prepared to stay in a dark room with no view on the back of the hotel.

8. Hotels detest any kind of eating in the room, so if you do, dispose of your papers, crumbs, and cores discreetly.

9. Never change money in a hotel, restaurant, or shop. Go to a bank for the best exchange rate. Never change on the black market—the money is counterfeit nine times out of ten.

10. Pack a Xeroxed copy of your passport, credit cards, airline tickets, hotel confirmation letters, and any other important documents without which you would be either in trouble or very inconvenienced.

11. Pickpockets are everywhere—and often when you least expect them. Carry your valuables in a money belt, or keep them locked up in a hotel safe.

12. Check out the hotel refund policy should you have to cancel a reservation. Some of the mom-and-pop pensiones have only one policy: You don't get your money back.

HIGH AND LOW SEASONS

Wouldn't it be wonderful to drop everything and fly to Italy whenever the spirit moved us? Unfortunately, most of us do not lead such charmed lives; instead we are bound by schedules, budgets, family considerations, and deadlines on all sides. To get the most out of your hotel dollar, the high and low seasons must be given serious attention.

Throughout Italy, the high seasons are generally from the first of April through October and the two weeks around Christmas and New Year's; Venice has an additional high season during the two weeks before Lent, when Carnevale is celebrated. August is the traditional vacation month for most in Rome, while in Venice vacation time is the damp months of January and February. In Florence, vacations seem to be spread out over the year, but Florentines observe the low seasons just as the Venetians and Romans do.

HOLIDAYS

January 1	New Year's Day
January 6	Epiphany
Easter	
Easter Monday	
April 25	Liberation Day
May 1	Labor Day
August 15	Assumption of the Virgin
November 1	All Saints' Day
December 8	Day of Immaculate Conception

December 25	Christmas
December 26	Santo Stefano
Patron Saints' Days	
Florence:	
June 24	St. John the Baptist's Day
Rome:	
June 29	St. Peter's Day
Venice:	
April 25	St. Mark's Day

On the eve of important holidays such as Christmas, New Year's, and Assumption, some stores close for the day at 1:00 P.M., and banks close at 11:30 A.M.

RESERVATIONS

People always ask me, "Do I need reservations?" The answer is *absolutely yes*, if you want to control your spending and stay within your budget. It is not unusual for hotels in Italy to be fully booked, even in the off seasons. Unless you do not mind taking a chance on a cancellation, paying more, or staying on the fringes, please make advance reservations. Today, the best way to reserve is by fax or telephone, followed by a guarantee with a major credit card or an international money order. No matter how you decide to make your reservations, the following points should be covered in your inquiry:

1. The dates of the stay, time of arrival, and number of people in the party.
2. The size and type of the room (double or twin beds, extra beds needed, adjoining rooms, suite, etc.).
3. The facilities needed: private toilet, shower and/or bathtub, or hall facilities if acceptable.
4. The location of the room: view, on the street, on the courtyard, or a quiet room on the back of the hotel.
5. The rates. Determine ahead what the nightly rate will be and state whether or not you will be eating breakfast at the hotel (you will save money if you do not). If you do not eat breakfast at the hotel, *be sure* it is deducted from the quoted rate.
6. The deposit required and the form of payment.

7. Request a confirmation in writing from the hotel for both your reservation and deposit, and carry this confirmation with you to the registration desk. You may have to show that there is a record of your reservation, or that you are not booked into a higher-priced room than you requested.

FAX

If you have a fax machine or access to one, and the hotel has a fax number, this is one of the best ways to make and confirm a reservation. To fax a message to Italy, use 011-39, then the city code (Florence: 55, Rome: 6, Venice: 41), and then the fax number of the hotel.

TELEPHONE

Always make the call during the hotel's weekday business hours to avoid talking to a night clerk who has limited authority to make advance reservations from abroad. Before calling, write down all your requests and questions. Ask the hotel to send you a written confirmation and, in turn, send them a letter confirming your telephone reservation. Send the letter certified, so you will know they received it, and keep a copy. In your letter to the hotel, cite the details of the conversation, the name of the person with whom you spoke, and the date and time of the call, and enclose a deposit if they do not accept a credit card number as a room guarantee. To dial direct to Italy from an AT&T phone, dial 011-39, then the city code and the number of the hotel. If you have another long-distance telephone service, check with them for their procedures for calling Italy.

TELEX

If you would prefer sending a telex and the hotel has a number, this is a cheap and reliable way to reserve because it gives you a record of your exchanges with the hotel. With the invention of the fax, however, fewer hotels have telex numbers. Given the choice between the two, always go with a fax.

LETTER

Everyone who has had any experience with the Italian mail service will tell you the same thing: It is, without question, terrible. Delays of up to two and three months are commonplace, and often mail simply does not reach its destination. If you insist on this old-fashioned way of reserving, allow plenty of time and expect long delays on both ends. Also, be prepared to leave on your trip without ever having heard from the three hotels you wrote to or, worse yet, to have corresponded with the hotel and to have sent the deposit, but never to have heard back. Believe me, this is *not* the way to travel in this wonderfully fast electronic world!

DEPOSITS

After making your reservations, most hotels will require at least a one-night deposit, even if you have been a guest there before. This is good insurance for both sides. The easiest way to handle a deposit is with a credit card. If the hotel does not take credit cards, there are other options. The next best thing is to send the hotel an international money order in U.S. dollars. This can be converted into Italian lire by the hotel and saves you having to get the money order in Italian lire on this side of the Atlantic. While this option is more convenient for you, it is added work and expense for the hotel, and those in the lower-priced categories will not do it—they will insist on a deposit made in Italian lire. Check with your local bank to see where you can obtain such a foreign-currency money order.

LATE ARRIVALS

Hotel guests are expected to arrive by 6:00 P.M. If you have a reservation, even with a deposit, the hotel does not always hold the room for you beyond this time unless they have been forewarned that you will be late. To allow for travel delays, always ask your hotel to hold your room for you, then call the minute you know you will be late. If arriving by plane or train, give the hotel the name of the airline and the flight number, or the train arrival time. Asking for the room to be held will oblige you to pay for it, even if you are delayed until the next morning—but believe me, it will be worth it in the long run.

MONEY MATTERS

If you remember to carry traveler's checks, charge big items on your credit card, convert to lire as you go, and use ATM's, you will do fine. Also, remember to carry a few of your own personal checks. If you suddenly run out of money, you can use them to get cash advances, provided the credit card you have allows this. Try to have a few lire on hand when you arrive. True, you may pay more for this convenience, but if you change only $200 before you leave home, you will never miss the few extra dollars it may cost against the convenience and peace of mind of having some money to tide you over until you can get to a bank.

ATM CARDS

If your ATM card is part of a network in the United States that also works abroad, you are in business. You use the machines in Italy the same as you do here, by punching in your personal identification (PIN) number and the amount of cash you want in local currency. You will benefit from the wholesale exchange rate banks use for large-scale transactions (sometimes up to 7 percent more favorable than at the bank for traveler's checks). Make sure your PIN number will be accepted in Italy. Your bank can confirm this, or change your number if necessary. Also ask your U.S. bank if any charges will be applied for using a foreign ATM. Finally, the strip on the back of ATM cards can become demagnetized, and therefore ineffectual, when passing through airport security checks and X-rays. Ask the security guard to hand-carry your card through the security check.

CREDIT CARDS

Despite the fact that Italy is the world's fifth-largest industrial nation, many hotels, restaurants, and shops have not kept pace with the rest of the world in accepting plastic instead of cash. This is *not*, however, a reason to leave your credit cards at home. Of course, you will leave all of your U.S. store credit cards at home, but you should take Visa, MasterCard, and/or American Express with you, as they are widely accepted throughout Italy. A credit card can be a lifesaver in emergencies when you need some quick cash, because most cards have instant cash advances. Check with your issuing bank for the conversion charges, interest rates, and credit limits on your account. Another reason for using plastic is that it eliminates the need for carrying large sums of cash, which must be purchased by standing in line at a bank or other money-changing facility. It also provides you with a record of your purchases, and, best of all, you often get delayed billing of up to four to six weeks after purchase. With a credit card, the money stays in your bank account, possibly drawing interest until you need it to pay the final bill. It is also important to remember that the currency conversion rate is made at the time of processing, not at the time of purchase by the consumer. Here are a few other tips on using credit cards:

1. If the dollar is not doing too well, use cash, including traveler's checks. On the other hand, if the dollar is going up, charge like crazy.

2. Before using your credit card, ask if there is any discount or incentive for paying in cash.

3. Keep a copy of all of your credit card numbers with you and leave another copy at home.

4. Save your receipts to check against the statement when it arrives. Errors are all too frequent.

5. Report the loss of your card immediately. Contact both the local police and the U.S. consular office. Leave a copy of your itinerary as well as your home address at both places on the chance that your credit card may turn up. When you get home, check your insurance policies to see if the loss is covered.

6. After reporting the loss to the police and consular office, report the loss to the credit card company. The following numbers will help:

American Express	1-800-528-4800 or 212-477-5700 (collect)
Diner's Club	1-800-525-9135 or 214-680-6480 (collect)
Master Card	314-275-6690 (collect)
Visa	415-574-7700 (collect)

7. Finally, emergency personal check–cashing is a benefit for many card holders, as is free car-rental insurance. Check with your issuing bank to determine the benefits you have—you may be pleasantly surprised.

PERSONAL CHECKS

Yes, you should take some with you. Personal checks are certainly not widely accepted, but some stores will take them and give you a better price than for credit cards, especially American Express, which is slow to pay the merchant and extracts a high commission. Also, you can use your checks to get cash advances with your credit cards at participating banks.

TRAVELER'S CHECKS

Banks offer the best exchange rate, much better than hotels or exchange windows that are identified by signs saying "Cambio," "Wechsel," or "Change." Estimate your needs carefully. If you overbuy in lire, you will lose twice, both in buying and in selling. Every time you change money, someone is making a profit, and I can guarantee that it is not you. You will always get a better rate for traveler's checks than for cash, but the real cost lies in what you spent to get the traveler's checks in the first place and what the commission is to cash them. If your bank gives free American Express traveler's checks, you can cash them commission-free at American Express offices anywhere in Italy. The drawback is that the lines are often long and slow. For the addresses of American Express offices in Florence, Rome, and Venice, see the information page for those cities.

Two final words of caution: *Never* change money on the Italian black market. The money is usually counterfeit. *Always* Xerox your passport and keep a separate record of your traveler's check numbers. These two precautions will save the day if your checks are lost or stolen.

Note: Italian banking hours are Monday through Friday from 8:30 A.M. to 1:30 P.M., and 3:00 or 3:30 to 4:00 or 4:30 P.M.

TIPPING

Tipping is definitely part of the Italian way of life and is expected on almost all levels of service. However, you are not required to tip if the service is poor or rude, or if the service is already included in your bill.

Beauty and barber shops	10–15% for each person who serves you
Caffès and bars	15% of bill if not already included
Hotels:	
Maids	L1,000 per day
Doorman for calling a taxi	L3,000
Bellboys and porters	L1,200 per bag
Concierge	L3,000 for each service given
Room service	L1,000
Restaurants	15% service is usually added to bill; if service has been exceptional, a few extra lire are always appreciated
Taxis	15% of fare
Theater usher	L1,500
Washroom attendants	L100–300

PACKING: DO YOU REALLY NEED ALL THAT?

Lay out all that you think you will need, then put half of it back into the closet. Trust me on this; you will be glad you did when you are lugging your suitcases up to that charming little pensione in Florence located on the fifth floor of a building with no elevator. Color-coordinate around one color, and use every nook and cranny of your suitcase to its fullest: Stuff your shoes; roll your sweaters; lay plastic garment bags between layers to prevent wrinkling, and pack the suitcase full so things will not slide to a pile at one end. Take clothes you would wear in any major metropolitan city. Short shorts, baseball caps, jogging outfits, and bare midriffs, no matter what the temperature is, will label you as a gauche tourist. Sleeveless dresses and bare chests are unwelcome in restaurants and in many museums and churches. Remember, you are not going to a deserted island, but to

Italy, where there are hundreds of shops selling everything you forgot to bring or may suddenly think you need. Besides, it is always fun to bring something home to wear that all of your friends can admire.

TELEPHONE

> Any country whose telephone numbers range from 4 to 8 digits has got to be exciting and full of surprises.
>
> —Michael Jackson

The wide range of digits in telephone numbers is just the start of the fun, fascination, and challenge of the Italian phone system. In Rome, telephone numbers can have 4, 5, 6, 7, or 8 digits. It is not quite as bad in Florence or Venice, but it is still not easy to master this tool that so many of us take for granted.

CALLS MADE WITHIN ITALY

If you make a long-distance call from a public telephone, there is no surcharge, but there can be one if you make the call from your hotel room. If you want to make a collect call or bill a call to your credit card, dial 170. An English-speaking operator will come on the line to assist you. To call the United States and Canada, dial 00 plus the country code (1 for the U.S. and Canada), the area code, and the number you are calling. Reduced rates are in effect from 11 P.M. to 8 A.M. on weekdays and all day on Sunday.

Long-distance operator in Italy

National	10
Europe and North Africa	15
Overseas	170
To USA via AT&T for calling card or collect	172 1011
To Canada via AT&T for calling card or collect	172 1001

CALLS MADE TO ITALY

To call Italy direct, dial 011-39, the city code, and then the number you are calling; when direct-dialing, drop the 0 from the city code (the zero is used only within Italy when calling from one city to another); for further information, call 1-800-874-4000.

Country code for Italy	39
City code for Florence	055
City code for Rome	06
City code for Venice	041

If you will be calling to and from Italy often, take advantage of the handy USA Direct Service offered by AT&T and MCI as well as by other telephone systems. Each company has a toll-free number that will connect you to an English-speaking operator who will place your call.

SAFETY

Caution and common sense should be exercised on a trip to Italy. It is best to leave all jewelry, expensive watches, and high-visibility wardrobes at home. Try to blend in. It is also a good idea to carry all valuables in a money belt or a necklace purse. If you do carry a purse, buy a sturdy one with a secure clasp and zipper, and carry it crosswise on the side of your body away from the street. Thieves on darting Vespas ride through the streets searching for likely victims. If you use a fanny pack, wear it in front, not in back. In cars, do not leave luggage locked inside, and open the door to the glove compartment to show potential thieves that nothing is there. If you are staying in a student accommodation, or in any place where you cannot lock up your valuables, always carry them on your person—*never* let them out of your sight, even if it means taking your camera and wallet with you to the showers. Watch out for Gypsy adults and children begging, and those on buses, the subway, and around tourist sites. All of these crafty pros will zero in on you. Steer clear of the children—they are the worst. They operate in a swarming mass with fluttering newspapers to divert your attention so that they can get in and out of your pocket before you know what hit you.

A FEW LAST-MINUTE HINTS

1. If you are the daredevil type and like putting your life on the line, you will love driving in Rome, where motorists drive with one hand on the horn, treat pedestrians as legitimate targets, and think of the road as a Grand Prix circuit.

2. In Rome, avoid the Via Veneto in the evening when hookers (who may or may not be female) and wallet-snatching Gypsy children make it an unsafe free-for-all.

3. As August nears, an exodus from Rome begins that rivals in magnitude Napoleon's retreat from Russia. Official estimates vary, but it is generally agreed that at least two thirds of the city's population leaves in August.

4. Use *only* legitimate taxis, not the maverick independents, no matter how cheap they quote a fare. If you are coming from the airport,

worries about flight safety fall by the roadside compared with the horrors of riding in a taxi driven by the Cabbie from Hell who listens to blaring tape recorders or radios, keeps the beat with the gas pedal, and turns his head in every direction but that of the road.

5. Before using a taxi, find out the starting rate that is legal where you are, and be sure that is the amount showing on the meter when you get in, or you may find yourself paying for someone else's ride.

6. For a successful trip kept within a budget, always *plan ahead*. Research where you want to go, how to get there, and the things you want to do along the way. Make hotel reservations to ensure that you get the hotel of your choice in the location you want and at the price you can afford to pay.

7. In Italy, a *piano* is not a musical instrument, it is a floor in a building. *Piano terra*, or T, means ground floor, and *primo piano*, or 1, means the first floor above the ground level.

8. It is not the washing of clothes that the hotels object to, it is the dripping. Wet clothes have ruined many carpets and stained many walls. If you must rinse out a few things, please let them drip dry over the tub, sink, or bidet. If you have jeans and other heavy articles to wash, inquire about the nearest coin-operated laundromat and use it. Hotel laundry services are sky-high, and so are finish laundries in all of the cities in *Cheap Sleeps in Italy*. Your best bet is to do it yourself and mix with the locals while your clothes are washing and drying. Who knows—it could turn out to be one of the more interesting times you have observing local color.

9. If you are staying in Florence from spring through fall, bring mosquito spray and a citronella candle. The mosquitos during this time of the year are lethal, and hotel window screens are nonexistent.

10. For a last-minute check on the weather in Italy before you leave the States, call 1-900-WEATHER. It costs just 75¢ a minute, and it gives hourly updated weather information and three-day accurate weather forecasts for 600 cities in the United States and the rest of the world.

How to Use
Cheap Sleeps in Italy

ABBREVIATIONS AND TERMS

The following abbreviations are used to denote which credit cards a hotel will accept:

American Express	AMEX
Diners Club	DC
MasterCard	MC
Visa	V

The following abbreviations are used after the listing of the number of rooms in each hotel to indicate the general type of bath and toilet facilities:

W/BST = number of rooms with private bath, shower, and toilet.
W/O BST = number of rooms without private facilities.

STARS

Hotels in Italy are controlled by a government rating system that ranks them from *no stars* to *four-star deluxe*. Every hotel must display prominently the number of stars it has.

A no-star hotel is basic, to put it mildly. A one-star hotel has minimum facilities. Two stars means a comfortable room with a telephone, but not necessarily an elevator. Three stars usually guarantees a private bathroom, a color TV, possibly air-conditioning, and perhaps an elevator. A four-star hotel is first class and has every comfort you will need.

Sometimes the number of stars in a lower category bears little relationship to the quality of service or facilities you will find. The stars do not correspond to the level of cleanliness or service, or the attitude of management and staff. In short, you cannot always judge a hotel by the number of stars it has.

ACCOMMODATIONS: CHECKING IN

When you arrive at the hotel, always ask to see the room assigned to you before approving it. If you are dissatisfied, ask to see another. After accepting the room, reconfirm the rate and whether or not you will be eating the hotel breakfast. If it is summertime, be sure that you know the cost of air-conditioning. In many two-star hotels, and some three, it is extra, and may be as much as 15,000 lire per day. This advance work prevents any unpleasant surprises when you check out.

The Italian hotel day begins and ends at noon. If you overstay, you could be charged the price of an extra day.

In most hotels, you pay for the room, not for the number of people in it. Thus, if you are alone and occupy a triple, you will pay the triple price. Most hotels have two kinds of double rooms: those with a double bed (*matrimoniale*) and those with twin beds (*due letti*). If you ask for a room with a bath, specify if you want a bathtub or will settle for a shower. Remember that showers cost less than bathtubs. When reserving, be specific about exactly what type of arrangements will suit you.

RATES: PAYING THE BILL

Hotel rates and the number of stars must be posted, and the rates *should* include all services and taxes.

Italian hotel rates are no longer tightly controlled by the government. As a result, hotels offer different rates at different times of the year, getting the most they can, even in the off seasons of the year. It always makes good Cheap Sleeping sense to ask for the lowest rate possible, and to go in an off season if your schedule permits.

All the rates listed in *Cheap Sleeps in Italy* are for full price and do not reflect special deals unless stated. While I have made every effort to be accurate on the rates, I cannot control dollar fluctuations or spiraling Italian inflation. So please be fully prepared to have the prices vary (unfortunately going up, not down).

All the hotel listings state which credit cards are accepted. In most Cheap Sleep listings, payment is required one night in advance to hold your room. Few low-priced hotels, youth hostels, or monastery dorms take credit cards. It is cash up front in Italian lire *only*. These hotels do not bend—so be prepared with cash when ready to check out.

Hotel exchange rates are notoriously low, and not in your best interest at all. If you must pay your bill in lire, convert your money at a bank before checking out.

Before leaving the hotel, go over your bill carefully, question anything you do not understand, and get a receipt marked *paid* before leaving.

BREAKFAST

Almost every hotel listed in *Cheap Sleeps in Italy* serves at least a Continental breakfast consisting of coffee, tea, hot chocolate, rolls, butter, and jam. Hotels stand to make an enormous profit on this meal and in some instances charge up to 25,000 lire per person. If you want anything extra, it costs dearly and is usually not worth the extra outlay. Many hotels are now offering a buffet with cereals, yogurt, meats, cheeses, and fruit added to the basic Continental meal. Sometimes the buffet is worth the price if you plan to skip lunch. If you are trying to save money, however, skip every hotel breakfast, insist that it be deducted from your bill, and join the locals standing at the corner *caffè*. You will have much more fun and save a bundle besides.

ENGLISH SPOKEN

All the listings indicate whether English is spoken. If you can dust off a few Italian phrases, smile, and display good will, you will find that the hotel staff will probably be warm and friendly and go out of their way to serve you. If you do not speak any Italian at all, it is important to know whether or not someone at the hotel speaks any English. While it is fun to practice your broken Italian, it is definitely not fun to be unable to communicate when facing a crisis.

FACILITIES AND SERVICES

A brief summary at the end of each hotel listing tells you which facilities and services the hotel offers. Of course, the more facilities, the more money you will have to spend. Please note that many Italian hotels do not have elevators. This does not mean that the hotel is not good. It probably means that it is situated in a historically designated building that does not allow the renovations necessary to install an elevator.

NEAREST TOURIST ATTRACTIONS AND AREA

Each hotel listing in the three cities covered tells you in which area of the city the hotel is located and states the tourist attractions that are within a reasonable walking distance.

FLORENCE

All saints can do miracles, but few of them can keep a hotel.
— Mark Twain
(Sign in a hotel in Florence, Italy)

Florence, the world's greatest celebration of the triumph of the human spirit, has long been regarded as the birthplace of the Renaissance and the Athens of modern civilization. Under the ruling of the powerful Medici family, Florence was decorated with churches and palaces, making it one of the greatest living museums in the world.

If you like to walk, you will love being in Florence, because almost everything a tourist wants to see and do is easy to manage on foot. You may explore her beautiful history by wandering down medieval streets and narrow lanes that have not changed in centuries. Wherever you turn, Florence is a feast for the eyes—whether you are looking at the River Arno and the Ponte Vecchio, or standing at Piazzale Michelangelo and gazing across the Arno over the red-tiled rooftops to the hazy Tuscan hills in the distance.

Many of the grand old villas of Florence have been made into hotels. These hotels range from simple pensiones with three or four rooms, to grand luxury palaces with every service you could want. Most are in ancient buildings that do not have elevators or modern plumbing, but that is part of the charm of staying in Florence and absorbing her special beauty.

The street addresses are different here, and that is an understatement if there ever was one. To the unknowing visitor, they can be impossible to figure out. Actually, once you get the system, they are easy to decipher. The addresses are numbered in red and black sequences. The red numbers are for commercial establishments (restaurants and shops) and the black are for residences and hotels. Black addresses will usually appear as a number only, while red addresses will appear as a number followed by the letter r. To add to the confusion, the numbers follow their own sequence. You will see 21r, 23r, 45, 47, and 49 all on the same side of the street in the same block. You just have to remember whether you are looking for a red or a black number.

USEFUL INFORMATION

Emergency	113
Ambulance, fire, police	112
First aid	212.222
Night doctor	477.891
A.V.O., or Associazione Volontari Ospedalieri	Volunteer interpreters who help with medical problems; Mon, Wed, and Fri 4–6 P.M.; 403.126 or 234.45.67
24-hour pharmacies, 7 days a week	Comunale, Train Station, track No. 6, 216.761 or 289.485; Molteni, Via Calzaiuoli, 7r, 215.472; Taverna, Piazza S. Giovanni, 20r, 284.013
Consulates	Great Britain, Lungarno Corsini, 2r, 284.133; United States, Lungarno Amerigo Vespucci, 38r, 298.276
Railway information	23.521 or 288.765
Train station luggage service	212.319
E.P.T.	Tourist information and complaints about hotels, Via Manzoni, 16r; Mon–Sat 8:30 A.M.–1:30 P.M.; 247.81.41
Currency exchange	Banks open 8:30 A.M.–1:30 P.M. and 2:45–3:45 P.M.; American Express, Via Guicciardini, 49r, Mon–Fri 9 A.M.–5:30 P.M., Sat 9 A.M.–12:30 P.M., 278.751; Esercizio Promozione Turismo will exchange money after banks close and on holidays; takes a commission, as do most banks; Via Condotta, 42r, 294.551
City telephone code for Florence	055

HOTELS IN FLORENCE BY AREA

BOBOLI GARDENS

Classic Hotel ★★★
Viale Machiavelli, 25

AREA
Boboli Gardens

TELEPHONE
(055) 229.351

FAX
(055) 229.353

TELEX
None

NUMBER OF ROOMS
20; all w/BST

CREDIT CARDS
AMEX, MC, V

RATES
Single L94,000; double L145,000; triple L198,000; suite for 2: L215,000; lower off-season rates Oct 31–March 1; breakfast included (if not eaten, deduct L9,000 per person)

Here is the quintessential Italian hotel, with high, molded ceilings, crystal chandeliers, inlaid hardwood floors, fireplaces, marble bathrooms, and lovely furniture that is in perfect keeping with the style of the hotel architecture. Set in an upscale residential area next to the Boboli Gardens, the Classic Hotel was a beautiful old villa until Connie Bernabei invested her heart, soul, and plenty of lire in turning it into one of the most alluring hotels in Florence. For some, the out-of-the-mainstream location might be a deterrent. But not for those who know and love Florence, because here you have the best of everything: peace and quiet in elegant parklike surroundings, and an easy 20-minute bus ride to absolutely everything on a tourist's itinerary in Florence. Motorists will also appreciate the free parking the hotel provides. All the rooms and bathrooms are stunning and spacious. A few favorites include No. 102, with a private balcony overlooking the street, and No. 101, a suite with a frescoed ceiling and a mezzanine bedroom with two double windows. Signora Bernabei offers a warm welcome to all of her guests and works tirelessly with her staff to make sure all of their needs are met. Her hotel receives my highest compliments and praise.

English Spoken: Yes

Facilities & Services: Bar, direct-dial phones, lift, free parking, room service, TV

Nearest Tourist Attractions: Boboli Gardens; 20-minute bus ride to everything in Florence

IL DUOMO

Albergo Firenze ★★
Piazza Donati, 4 (Via del Corso)

AREA
Il Duomo

For a central location within easy walking distance to just about everything a tourist might want to see and do in Florence, reserve a room at the two-star Albergo Firenze. The house has a famous past. In the 13th century it was the home of the powerful Donati family and the birthplace of Gemma Donati, wife of Dante Alighieri. Now a gradual renovation project is in progress. When it is completed, all the rooms will have private bathrooms and air-conditioning. Even though the older rooms are large and nicely furnished, for the little extra per night I would book a new room, because at least five or six of the older, bathless rooms must share the hall facilities. The new rooms are nicely done, with modern walnut furniture consisting of a desk and chair, a bureau, and two bedside chests. Above all, the hotel is quiet, despite its central location.

English Spoken: Yes

Facilities & Services: Air-conditioning in rooms with private baths; direct-dial phones; hair dryers in rooms with private baths; lift; TV in newer rooms, otherwise L4,000 per day

Nearest Tourist Attractions: Il Duomo; can walk to most everything else

TELEPHONE
(055) 268.301 or 214.203

FAX
(055) 212.370

TELEX
None

NUMBER OF ROOMS
60; w/BST, 25; w/o BST, 35

CREDIT CARDS
None

RATES
Single L41,000–55,000; double L70,000–80,000; triple L95,000–110,000; quad L120,000–135,000; breakfast included

Grand Hotel Cavour ★★★
Via del Proconsolo, 3b

If you like elegant surroundings with all the services and extras, then you will love the Grand Hotel Cavour, directly opposite the Bargello Museum in the heart of Florence. The hotel is a former 13th-century palace built by the Cerchi family. At the end of the 19th century it became a leading hotel, and it remains so to this day.

Despite renovations and changes over the years, the hotel has kept its architectural heritage and is truly magnificent throughout. The old chapel with its altar and confessional still intact is now the Ristorante Beatrice. The beautifully hand-painted ceilings, original stained-glass windows, and gleaming silverware create an air of refined luxury in this fine restaurant. For guests at the hotel, half-board for either lunch or dinner is available. The dramatic lounge has polished marble floors, a fountain in one

AREA
Il Duomo

TELEPHONE
(055) 282.461, toll-free from U.S. & Canada 1-800-448-8355

FAX
(055) 218.955

TELEX
580318 Cavour 1

NUMBER OF ROOMS
89; all w/BST

CREDIT CARDS
AMEX, DC, MC, V

RATES
Single L130,000; double L205,000; triple L280,000; half-board in restaurant L160,000–205,000 per person; breakfast L25,000, included

corner, massive gold mirrors, and stunning sectional sofas especially designed for the room. The comfortable bedrooms keep pace with the rest of the hotel. They are uniformly done, with rose-colored carpets, walnut furniture, and coordinated spreads and curtains. They have large closets, good drawer and luggage space, and beautiful baths fully stocked with toiletries and outfitted with heated towel racks, large fluffy towels, and tubs polished to perfection. On every floor there is a room with a bath especially equipped for the handicapped.

On the sixth floor is the Michelangelo breakfast room and adjoining terrace, with a panoramic view of Florence. A large buffet breakfast is served either inside or out, depending on the weather. The breakfast costs L25,000 per person, so you might consider going elsewhere at least part of the time, if management will agree to deduct this high-cost meal from your bill.

English Spoken: Yes

Facilities & Services: Air-conditioning, bar, direct-dial phones, dining room, hair dryers in most bathrooms, lift, mini-bars, parking can be arranged, room service, TVs, laundry service

Nearest Tourist Attractions: Within walking distance of everything Florence has to offer

Hotel Aldini ★★
Via Calzaiuoli 13

AREA
Il Duomo

TELEPHONE
(055) 214.752 or 212.448

FAX
(055) 216.410 per Aldini

TELEX
580252 per Aldini

NUMBER OF ROOMS
15; all w/BST

CREDIT CARDS
MC, V

RATES
Single L85,000; double L140,000; triple L195,000; breakfast included

The Aldini shows the marks of uniform good taste and the knowledge of how to run a good hotel. It also receives high honors for comfortable accommodations in a desirable location that is about as central as you will get in Florence. The clean white rooms are freshly painted and have copies of dark Italian country furniture and terra-cotta floors. Floral-print spreads in green, gold, and orange give a needed bright splash of color, and matching orange fabric–covered headboards tie everything together. For longer stays, there is good wardrobe and drawer space. To buffer any noise, the windows are double-glazed, and to keep you cool in the sizzling summer months, rooms are fully air-conditioned. The management is attentive without being familiar.

English Spoken: Yes

Facilities & Services: Air-conditioning, direct-dial phones, lift to hotel on third floor, TVs

Nearest Tourist Attractions: Central Florence; convenient to everything on foot

Hotel Brunori ★
Via del Proconsolo, 5

English-speaking owners Giovanni and Leonardo go out of their way to be helpful to their guests. They are always on board to see that all goes well with the day-to-day running of their nine-room hotel, so conveniently located right in the middle of Florence. The rooms are sparsely furnished with modern beds, tables, hard chairs, and small reading lamps. You won't be subjected to wild fabrics and mismatched prints here; everything is just plain and simple, with no extras. True Cheap Sleepers might want to ask for a room without the cost of a shower, towels, and breakfast added. From this perch on the pedestrian-only Via Proconsolo, you are within a 10- to 20-minute walk to everything on your list of things to do in Florence.

English Spoken: Yes

Facilities & Services: None; lockout at 12:30 A.M.

Nearest Tourist Attractions: Central to almost everything

AREA
Il Duomo

TELEPHONE
(055) 289.648

FAX
None

TELEX
None

NUMBER OF ROOMS
9; w/BST, 1; w/o BST, 8

CREDIT CARDS
None

RATES
Single L33,000–42,000; double L59,000–66,000; triple L80,000–95,000; towels L1,500 in rooms with no bath; showers L3,000; breakfast L7,000 extra

Hotel Calzaiuoli ★★★
Via Calzaiuoli, 6

If you pinpointed the best central location in Florence, anything on the pedestrian-only Via Calzaiuoli would come up a winner. At this restored 46-room hotel, once you get by the boring commercial lobby and lounge and see the original stone staircase and the handsome halls lined in muted wallpaper, you will be home free. In addition to space, a rarity in most hotels in this old section of Florence, the streamlined rooms have fabric-covered walls with matching curtains and bedspreads, and tile

AREA
Il Duomo

TELEPHONE
(055) 212.456/7/8

FAX
(055) 268.310

TELEX
508589

NUMBER OF ROOMS
46; all w/BST

CREDIT CARDS
AMEX, MC, V
RATES
Single L98,000; double
L150,000; extra bed L35,000;
breakfast L12,000 extra

bathrooms that would pass any compulsive housekeeper's cleanliness tests. A high-priced breakfast is served in the formal dining room, which has banquette seating highlighted by linen-clad tables, monogrammed china, and bouquets of fresh flowers. Dedicated Cheap Sleepers will probably want to go elsewhere for their morning repast. There are loads of nice *caffès* in the immediate vicinity, and I recommend them over the hotel dining room for both atmosphere and price. From many of the rooms you will have good views directly onto the street. This is a traffic-free zone, so you will be able to fine-tune your people-watching skills from your window instead of lying awake at night counting horn honks and backfires from racing mopeds.

English Spoken: Yes

Facilities & Services: Air-conditioning, bar, direct-dial phones in rooms and baths, hair dryers, lift, mini-bars, private room safes, TVs with satellite reception including CNN, laundry service

Nearest Tourist Attractions: Dead center to almost everything in Florence

Hotel Orchidea ★
Borgo degli Albizi, 11

AREA
Il Duomo
TELEPHONE
(055) 248.03.46
FAX
None
TELEX
None
NUMBER OF ROOMS
7; 1 with shower only,
all others w/o BST
CREDIT CARDS
None
RATES
Single L35,000; double
L51,000; quad L100,000;
breakfast not served

Maria Rosa Cook, a former English teacher, and her daughter Miranda run the cozy Hotel Orchidea. The 12th-century building overlooks Gemma's Tower, named after Gemma Donati, the wife of Dante, Italy's greatest poet. This tower can be seen from the nearby S. Pier Maggiore square, which is one of the most characteristic in this part of Florence.

The seven-room, first-floor lodging offers exceptionally clean, large rooms painted in a soft pink shade. Several have quiet views of the garden below with its leafy green planting. The area around the hotel is interesting because, in addition to being close to all the tourist musts, there is good shopping, from the Standa Department Store at the corner (the K-Mart of Italy), to artists' boutiques, newsstands, and fruit stalls. Reservations in the high seasons are difficult, so if this is your spot, plan far in advance.

English Spoken: Yes
Facilities & Services: Lift to hotel
Nearest Tourist Attractions: Santa Croce, Il Duomo, good shopping

Maria Luisa de' Medici ★
Via del Corso, 1

The Maria Luisa de' Medici has a faded elegance about it that will appeal to artistic types who love retro clothing discovered in out-of-the-way thrift stores. Each eccentric room is named after one of the last dukes of the Medici and is adorned with one of their portraits. The rooms display an eclectic mixture of almost-antiques and funky modern stuff that has been collected by one of the owners. There is a dust ball or two in sight once in a while, but generally speaking, they are clean enough for everyone except maybe your maiden Aunt Cora. The atmosphere of the hotel can best be described as chummy, since eight rooms must use two hall bathrooms. A large breakfast that includes juice, cereal, yogurt, eggs, and a choice of breads and cheese is served in your room each morning. With all this food, you should be fine until dinner, with maybe a *gelato* in the afternoon to tide you over. Usually, hotel rooms along this traffic-free prime patch of real estate cost a pretty lira, but for three or four people traveling together and willing to share one of the enormous family rooms with its own bathroom, the price is very attractive, especially when you consider the size of the breakfast.

English Spoken: Yes
Facilities & Services: Air-conditioning in 3 rooms, L10,000 per room
Nearest Tourist Attractions: Piazza della Repubblica, Il Duomo, Central Market, Uffizi Gallery, Ponte Vecchio

AREA
Il Duomo
TELEPHONE
(055) 280.048
FAX
None
TELEX
None
NUMBER OF ROOMS
10; w/BST, 2; w/o BST, 8
CREDIT CARDS
None
RATES
1 or 2 persons L80,000; triple or quad L38,000–45,000 per person; breakfast included

PIAZZA DELLA LIBERTÀ

Hotel Royal ★★★
Via delle Ruote, 52

The Hotel Royal is a magnificent turn-of-the-century private villa set off the street in a large

AREA
Piazza della Libertà

TELEPHONE
(055) 495.274, 483.287, or
490.648

FAX
(055) 490.976

TELEX
None

NUMBER OF ROOMS
41; all w/BST

CREDIT CARDS
AMEX, MC, V

RATES
Single L150,000; double
L225,000; triple L310,000;
breakfast included

manicured garden not far from the train station. Beautifully redone and professionally managed, this is one of the best three-star picks in Florence—and worth every extra lira it costs. Light gray and soft blue walls accented with white molding, massive crystal chandeliers, highly polished hardwood floors with Oriental rugs, a cozy circular bar, and strategically arranged chairs for quiet conversations create a lovely sitting room overlooking the back garden. In the spring and summer, breakfast is served in the garden, which is filled with roses and other blooming plants. At other times of the year, it is served in a glassed-in dining room that overlooks the garden. The quiet bedrooms are a tour-de-force of well-planned decor and comfort. All are large and invite long, lingering stays. Most have large shuttered windows with floor-to-ceiling white linen curtains gently pulled back to let in just enough sunshine. The rooms are perfectly quiet and have views of the garden. Framed French botanical prints, excellent lighting, and roomy bathrooms add the touches that make the difference between just a place to sleep and a memorable hotel experience you will remember long after other details of the trip fade.

English Spoken: Yes

Facilities & Services: Air-conditioning, bar, direct-dial phones, hair dryers, lift, mini-bars, free parking, TVs with satellite reception

Nearest Tourist Attractions: None; must walk 10 minutes or take a bus

PIAZZALE DI PORTA AL PRATO

Hotel Villa Azalee ★★★
Viale Fratelli Roselli, 44

AREA
Piazzale di Porta al Prato

TELEPHONE
(055) 214.242 or 284.331

FAX
(055) 268.264

TELEX
None

NUMBER OF ROOMS
25; all w/BST

It is always hard to be objective when you are in love, and I fell in love with the Villa Azalee the minute I saw it.

The hotel is done with great taste and style, and no effort has been spared to create a haven of beauty and charm. It has that small-hotel look and feel, which is achieved through an imaginative personal touch and a dedicated staff committed to what they are doing and willing to go the extra mile to provide service to each guest.

The floral-motif bedrooms vary, but all are simply wonderful, especially No. 29, with a pink wrought-iron four-poster bed with a frilly ruffle around the top. The room overlooks a garden blooming with seasonal plants and bushes. Number 21 faces the street in the main building. The double bed has a canopy hung from the ceiling, and there is a big chaise just perfect for snuggling into with a good book. Downstairs is a glassed-in sunroom and another, more formal room, around the corner. Both are filled with attractive furniture, green plants, and an abundance of easy chairs and sofas. Breakfast is served in an adorable room with pink and blue quilted slipcovers over ladderbacked chairs. If you don't want to come down for breakfast, call for room service.

Despite its rather distant location from central Florence, there is excellent bus service just around the corner.

Note: If you are a light sleeper, consider earplugs, because some of the rooms face a busy street with 24-hour traffic. The windows are double-glazed, but sometimes it isn't enough, or you may want to have the windows open. The rooms on the garden are quiet.

English Spoken: Yes

Facilities & Services: Air-conditioning, bar, direct-dial phones, hair dryers, mini-bars, garage L25,000 per day, room service, TVs

Nearest Tourist Attractions: None; must use public transportation

Hotel San Remo ★★★
Lungarno Serristori, 13

Sometimes the best hotels I have found for the Cheap Sleeps series have been by pure good fortune. Such was the case with the Hotel San Remo, which I walked by on a rainy Sunday afternoon in Florence. The San Remo is a three-star riverside site that will appeal to those voyagers in search of more for less.

CREDIT CARDS
AMEX, DC, MC, V

RATES
Single L120,000;
double L180,000; larger rooms L250,000; breakfast included

AREA
Piazzale Michelangelo

TELEPHONE
(055) 234.28.23/4

FAX
(055) 234.2269

TELEX
None

NUMBER OF ROOMS
20; all w/BST

CREDIT CARDS
AMEX, DC, MC, V

RATES
Single L98,000; double
L150,000; triple L190,000;
quad L230,000; breakfast
included (if not eaten, deduct
L8,500 per person)

For me, the bottom line on a hotel (besides the price) is always: How clean is it? I can assure you the San Remo scores a perfect ten, with no cracks, peeling paint, telltale odors, or creeping mildew. Owned and run with great pride and dedication by the Montagnani family for almost 30 years, the hotel is well kept, with guest comfort and all the little details that count put first. I especially like room No. 25, with pink floral wallpaper and lacy window curtains. Pretty Florentine metal bed lights, several nice paintings, and three decent chairs add to its appeal. Number 29 has a small entry hall, built-in closets, a quilted paisley bedspread, and a river view. The basement dining room is interesting, with its original brick curved ceiling exposed. Beyond this is a sitting room with a fireplace, low leather arm chairs, and a long trestle table. Upstairs is another sitting room, but guests seem to gather here, especially when there is a significant sporting event on the television. If the hotel were slightly more central, the rates would be *much* higher. But, within a 10-minute walk you can be at the Ponte Vecchio, and within 20, standing on the Piazza Santa Spirito or admiring the paintings in the Pitti Palace.

English Spoken: Yes

Facilities & Services: Air-conditioning, bar, direct-dial phones, hair dryers, lift, TVs

Nearest Tourist Attractions: Other side of Arno: Ponte Vecchio, Pitti Palace, Piazza Santa Spirito (20 minutes)

PIAZZA MASSIMO D'AZEGLIO

Hotel Genève ★
Via della Mattonaia, 43

AREA
Piazza Massimo d'Azeglio

TELEPHONE
(055) 247.79.23 or 247.80.62

FAX
None

TELEX
None

At the Pensione Genève, if you reserve a room for two with a shower and eat breakfast, you will not think you are getting a Cheap Sleep and you will be correct. However, if you breakfast elsewhere and bunk in a bathless room, your sleep will be much cheaper. The rooms are done à la one star, i.e., the bedspreads do not always match the decor and the furniture is Early Garage Sale Gothic. The difference here is that the spotless rooms are large enough for you and a suitcase or two.

Most small hotels have a few watercolors or oils displayed in the lounge or the dining room. Here you are treated to owner Signora Grazzia's noteworthy collection, which she hangs throughout the hotel. Be sure to take a minute or two to admire them. The major drawback for many will be the fringe location, which is a 20- or 30-minute walk to the center of the tourist action in Florence. Bus service is, of course, faster. However, the neighborhood is typical, and there is a nice park nearby for picnic lunches or just lazy people-watching.

English Spoken: Yes

Facilities & Services: Bar, direct-dial phones, dining room with meals for groups only (arrangements must be made when reserving)

Nearest Tourist Attractions: None; must use public transportation or walk

NUMBER OF ROOMS
12; w/BST, 10; w/o BST, 2

CREDIT CARDS
V

RATES
Single L48,000; double L81,000–95,000; triple L127,000; breakfast included (if not eaten, deduct L10,000 per person)

PIAZZA SAN MARCO

Hotel Splendor ★★★
Via San Gallo, 30

The Hotel Splendor recently has been awarded a third star, and no wonder. The family-owned hotel occupying the top three floors of an apartment building in a residential neighborhood is splendid in every respect. As you approach the building, look for the flowering window boxes on the nine windows that face the street. You enter through large doors and walk up a flight of carpeted stone steps to the reception desk, where you will be greeted by a member of the Masoero family.

The sitting room, with its large television, arm chairs nicely covered in floral fabric, and a lovely chandelier hanging from a magnificent 150-year-old hand-painted ceiling, is an inviting place to while away an hour or so. Breakfast can be served on the sunny terrace, where you can listen to the chimes from the San Marco church, or in the dining room, which has original murals on the walls. Not all of the

AREA
Piazza San Marco

TELEPHONE
(055) 483.427

FAX
(055) 461-276

TELEX
None

NUMBER OF ROOMS
31; w/BST, 23; w/o BST, none

CREDIT CARDS
MC, V

RATES
Single L85,000; double L110,000–140,000; triple L155,000–185,000; quad L195,000–230,000; breakfast buffet included

rooms are alike or are filled with antiques you wish you owned, although now that the hotel has three stars, that will be changing. However, the rooms are quiet, perfectly maintained, and large enough for a long, relaxed stay. I like No. 24, with its inlaid floor, new bath, high ceilings, and a bright exposure. Number 30 is a top-floor twin with turn-of-the-century twin beds on claw feet, and a matching dresser and armoire. A wall of windows lets in plenty of light all day long.

English Spoken: Yes

Facilities & Services: Air-conditioning in some, direct-dial phones, 1 A.M. lockout

Nearest Tourist Attractions: Accademia Gallery; 20-minute walk to Central Market and Il Duomo

Il Guelfo Bianco ★★★
Via Cavour, 57

AREA
Piazza San Marco

TELEPHONE
(055) 288.330

FAX
(055) 295.203

TELEX
570596 Guelfo I

NUMBER OF ROOMS
21; all w/BST

CREDIT CARDS
AMEX, MC, V

RATES
Single L126,000–160,000; double L182,000; triple L250,000; quad L305,000; large Continental breakfast included

An up-market, midtown choice, Il Guelfo Bianco is ideal for those wanting to be a heartbeat away from the artistic and architectural treasures of Florence. For the businessman, it is within a short taxi ride to the Exhibition and Convention Center. For the shopper, call it Mecca.

The hotel has been totally redone from stem to stern, and the results are dramatic. The bedrooms are small, but furnished with a sense of imagination and style. All are soundproofed and air-conditioned, a true blessing in the summer, when temperatures rise and the mosquitos arrive. The rooms are uniformly done in shades of green, with coordinated carpets and draperies. The beautiful bathrooms have nice fixtures and good lighting, and are large enough to turn around in and lay out a few things. A summer breakfast is served under umbrellas in an inner courtyard. During the winter, it is served in a breakfast room with a vase of dried flowers set on each damask-clad table. Management, under the guidance of owner Luisa Ginti, is young and enthusiastically professional.

English Spoken: Yes

Facilities & Services: Air-conditioning, bar, direct-dial phones, hair dryers, lift, mini-bars, parking can be arranged, private room safes, laundry service, TVs and radios.

Nearest Tourist Attractions: Piazza San Marco, Piazza SS. Annunziata, Il Duomo, Central Market

PIAZZA SANTA MARIA NOVELLA

Hotel Aprile ★★★
Via della Scala, 6

The Aprile has been preserved by the Commission of Fine Arts as a historic monument. Converted from a 15th-century Medici palace, it retains its original frescoes and hand-decorated vaulted ceilings. Because of its busy location, there is noise, but if you are on the back side, uninterrupted sleep will be possible. It is not a spacious hotel, but that does not take away from its overall appeal. Downstairs is a modest reception area, a lounge, and a bar, all filled with lovely green plants. The bar has an arched ceiling and comfortable red velvet chairs scattered among leather couches and arm chairs. Breakfast is served in a room with a ceiling dating from the 1700s and chairs nicely upholstered in pink petit point. On warm mornings, you can enjoy your cappuccino and rolls in the garden next to it. Upstairs the rooms are big enough, scrupulously clean, and decked out with tiled baths and walnut or wrought-iron furniture, and many have a view of the Piazza Santa Maria Novella. Number 9 can be either a double or triple. It has a built-in armoire, a garden view, a pull-down desk, two arm chairs, and a sofa that can be made into a bed for a third person. The ceiling is painted a beautiful blue with a soft floral trim. A blue cotton spread on the wrought-iron bed and good bedside reading lights round out the package. If you are here in an off season and forego the breakfast, this three-star hotel with all the trimmings is a great deal.

English Spoken: Yes

Facilities & Services: Bar, direct-dial phones, lift, mini-bars, room service for breakfast and bar drinks

Nearest Tourist Attractions: Piazza Santa Maria Novella, Arno, Il Duomo; almost everything on this side of river is within walking distance

AREA
Piazza Santa Maria Novella

TELEPHONE
(055) 216.237 or 289.147

FAX
(055) 280.947

TELEX
575.840

NUMBER OF ROOMS
29; w/BST, 25; w/o BST, 4

CREDIT CARDS
AMEX, MC, V

RATES
Single L70,000–110,000; double L100,000–160,000; lower off-season rates; breakfast included, but can be deducted

Hotel Visconti ★
Piazza degli Ottaviani, 1

AREA
Piazza Santa Maria Novella

TELEPHONE
(055) 213.877

FAX
None

TELEX
None

NUMBER OF ROOMS
10; w/BST, 4; w/o BST, 6

CREDIT CARDS
None

RATES
Single L33,000–45,000;
double L50,000–65,000;
triple L65,000–80,000;
breakfast L12,000 extra

Manara Gaetano is an architect who has owned this little one-star hotel for seven years. Before that he lived in Idaho and Washington, so you can be sure his English is perfect, down to the last idiom. As an architect, he naturally had all the say in designing the interior of his hotel. The best part is the lighted terrace, where he serves either an Italian or American breakfast. If you order Italian, you will have cheese, cakes, fruit salad, and fresh rolls along with your strong coffee. The American breakfast offers cheese, eggs, yogurt, and weak American-style coffee.

Blue and white is the color theme used throughout the hotel. The small windowless sitting room has stark white Roman statuary positioned against a Williamsburg-blue backdrop. Rooms have white wipe-off furniture, clean bathrooms with shower curtains, hardwood floors, and coordinated wall coverings and fabrics. If you are willing to stay in a bathless room and breakfast elsewhere, this is a top-drawer Cheap Sleep.

English Spoken: Yes

Facilities & Services: Air-conditioning L3,000 per room, portable heat L3,000 per room, lift

Nearest Tourist Attractions: Il Duomo, Arno; can walk to train station

Pensione Ottaviani ★
Piazza Ottaviani, 1 (corner of Piazza Santa Maria Novella)

AREA
Piazza Santa Maria Novella

TELEPHONE
(055) 239.62.23

FAX
None

TELEX
None

NUMBER OF ROOMS
12; w/BST, 4; w/o BST, 8

CREDIT CARDS
None

This pensione is run by an elderly couple who rule the roost from their perches behind the reception desk. If you stay here you can count on clean rooms with no musty odors. There is a lift from the ground floor up to the second floor where the pensione is located. A 12:30 A.M. curfew and lockout is emphatically enforced. If you stay out past that time, you won't be sleeping here. The best part about this one is that the prices are gentle and kind to those on a budget, especially during the low season. The rooms are uniform in their total simplicity. The paint is reasonably fresh, the colors match well enough, and the linoleum floors are washed every day. The back rooms on the top floor are the best. If you are any place along the front, bring earplugs, because the traffic is like a race track day and night. The bathrooms are basic, and most are behind folding doors. If you stay in a bathless room you will shower in a room with only a shower spout and a drain, no curtain. But this is Italy, and shower curtains are not standard bathroom equipment. Breakfast is served in a cheery ten-tabled breakfast room facing the street.

English Spoken: Enough

Facilities & Services: Lift

Nearest Tourist Attractions: Within walking distance of almost everything; minutes from the train station, where you can get a bus if you don't want to walk where you are going

RATES
Single L39,000–48,000; double L53,000–70,000; triple L100,000; lower rates during off season; breakfast included

PIAZZA SANTO SPIRITO

Istituto Gould (no stars)
Via dei Serragli, 49

The Istituto Gould was founded by American Emily Gould in 1872. Today it is part of the Protestant Church of Italy and is a home for boys and girls from eight to 18 who, because of severe family problems (not drugs), cannot live with their own families. On the second floor in the Florence location, the institute operates a type of hostel open to anyone all year long. In doing my research for the Cheap Sleeps series I have seen my share of hostels, but let me assure you, this one resembles a hostel like a Rolls-Royce does a bicycle—in other words, it is a standout. One side is admittedly newer. Although none of them are lavish, all of the crisply modern and functional rooms are clean and very neat. There are no hideous color mismatches, no unsightly tears, and no tacky furniture.

Five rooms open onto a lovely shared terrace; others overlook the institute's gardens and Fort Belvedere in the distance. Meal service is available for groups of 20 or more. The best part, I think, about

AREA
Piazza Santo Spirito

TELEPHONE
(055) 212.576

FAX
(055) 280.274

TELEX
None

NUMBER OF ROOMS
25; w/BST, 20; w/o BST, 5

CREDIT CARDS
None

RATES
Single L35,000; double L25,000 per person; breakfast not included (served only to groups)

staying here is that the money received goes directly to the institute to help the children. What better way to spend your hotel lire?

English Spoken: Yes

Facilities & Services: None; meals can be provided for groups of 20 or more

Nearest Tourist Attractions: Piazza Santo Spirito, Pitti Palace

Pensione Sorelle Bandini ★
Piazza Santo Spirito, 9

AREA
Piazza Santo Spirito

TELEPHONE
(055) 215.318

FAX
None

TELEX
None

NUMBER OF ROOMS
10; w/BST, 5; w/o BST, 5

CREDIT CARDS
None

RATES
1 or 2 persons L83,000–95,000; triple L116,000–133,000; quad L150,000–175,000; breakfast included, but L15,000 can be deducted per person Nov–Jan

Warning: This is not a hotel for everyone. Guests either fiercely defend it, or would not stay here again if you gave them the room for free. If you like shiny chrome and glass, slick bathrooms, and heel-clicking service, better skip this one. On the other hand, if you like a laid-back management, appreciate slightly wrinkled and faded charm, love large view rooms filled with massive antiques in need of some elbow grease, and enjoy reading or napping on verandas with sweeping views of the Piazza Santo Spirito, then you will be a fan of the Bandini. It does have other drawbacks. The housekeeping staff could use some reminders, especially in the hall toilets and showers, and maintenance is definitely in the deferred category. Breakfast is included in the price, but if you are here from November through January, it will be deducted at the rate of L15,000 *per person*!

English Spoken: Yes

Facilities & Services: None

Nearest Tourist Attractions: Piazza Santo Spirito, Pitti Palace, Ponte Vecchio

PIAZZA SS. ANNUNZIATA

Hotel Loggiato dei Serviti ★★★
Piazza SS. Annunziata, 3

AREA
Piazza SS. Annunziata

TELEPHONE
(055) 289.592/3/4, 219.165, or 239.82.80

The Loggiato dei Serviti occupies one of the city's most beautiful Renaissance buildings on the Piazza SS. Annunziata. The hotel was not always as wonderful as it is now, believe me! Years ago I stayed here when it was a dilapidated no-star pensione. I have vivid memories of the several sleepless summer nights I spent swatting kamikaze mosquitos and lying under damp towels in an effort to keep cool. When I was in Florence this time to do the research for *Cheap Sleeps in Italy*, I learned that the hotel had recently been sold and undergone a total transformation. This was one I *had* to see. I am happy to say that now, thanks to meticulous restoration by the Budini-Gatti family, the Loggiato is an elegant and tranquil place to stay, with every modern convenience. The 16th-century architecture of the building has been left unchanged, and everything about the hotel fits right into the spirit of its heritage as a former monastery. The lovely breakfast room, polished terra-cotta floors, hand-colored prints on the walls, magnificent dried and fresh floral arrangements, and enviable Italian antiques throughout will carry you back to an era when graciousness and etiquette mattered. Each of the bedrooms has its own individual character. Some, particularly the singles, are small, with bathrooms squeezed into corners and closet space cut to the minimum. Many other rooms, however, are large, especially No. 31, a two-room suite with a spacious sitting room and a view of Il Duomo. Because the Loggiato is now so well done and nicely run, I am happy to recommend it to those who are looking for a special hotel with the true feel of Florence.

English Spoken: Yes

Facilities & Services: Air-conditioning, bar, direct-dial phones, hair dryers, mini-bars, lift, garage service L42,000 per day, private room safes, TVs

Nearest Tourist Attractions: Church of SS. Annunziata, Foundling's Hospital, Il Duomo, Central Market, San Marco Square and Church, Accademia Gallery

Hotel Morandi alla Crocetta ★★★
Via Laura, 50

The Morandi alla Crocetta, an absolute jewel, combines the best of modern comfort with the warmth of antique furnishings in an exquisitely restored convent dating to 1511. At this quiet and

FAX
(055) 289.595

TELEX
575808 LOGSER I

NUMBER OF ROOMS
29; all w/BST

CREDIT CARDS
AMEX, DC, MC, V

RATES
Single L140,000; double L210,000; triple L285,000; suite for 4 L375,000–475,000; breakfast included

AREA
Piazza SS. Annunziata

TELEPHONE
(055) 234.47.47
FAX
(055) 248.09.54
TELEX
None
NUMBER OF ROOMS
9; all w/BST
CREDIT CARDS
AMEX, DC, MC, V
RATES
Single L95,000; double
L150,000; triple L195,000;
breakfast L15,000 extra

distinguished hotel, the staff prides themselves on giving four-star service and personal attention to all of their guests. English owner Katherine Doyle employs her own staff of carpenters, who are working carefully and slowly to restore this lovely building. Exposed parts of the original structure, the ingenious use of pieces from other old buildings, and authentic antiques work together to create a charming hotel with a definite sense of its past. As you enter from the street, you pass by two large red clay pots and walk up the red-carpeted stairway to the front door to ring the bell. You will be ushered into a comfortable sitting room where easy chairs are well placed for conversation or for just sitting and reading the morning paper. The rooms vary in size and magnitude, but all are brilliantly conceived. One of the best is the chapel, with original frescoes that show the artist's brush strokes. Number 1 is a double, with four pieces of Mass vestments framed and hung as backdrops for the bed. Number 29, a suite, has exposed arches and 16th-century frescoes depicting the life of the nun who founded the convent in the days of Lorenzo de' Medici.

As you can imagine, once people discover the Morandi, they never want to stay anyplace else. With only nine rooms, reservations fill up quickly, so you *must* plan far ahead to stay here.

English Spoken: Yes

Facilities & Services: Air-conditioning, direct-dial phones, hair dryers, mini-bars, private room safes, TVs with satellite and CNN, radios

Nearest Tourist Attractions: Accademia Gallery, Piazza SS. Annunziata, Archeological Museum

PONTE VECCHIO

Aily Home ★
Piazza Stefano, 1

AREA
Ponte Vecchio

A stay at the Aily Home may not make you feel pampered, but you will feel safe and, above all, proud to be saving so much money that you can spend in other ways. This four-room, third-floor walk-up is convenient to the Uffizi Gallery and the Ponte Vecchio, shopping, and good restaurants (see *Cheap Eats in Italy* for suggestions). The rooms are dark but clean, and the furniture is relatively modern. All four rooms in the pensione must share one hall toilet and shower. No breakfast is served. As you can see, this is definitely nothing special, but it *is* too cheap to ignore.

English Spoken: No

Facilities & Services: None

Nearest Tourist Attractions: Ponte Vecchio, Uffizi Gallery, Arno

TELEPHONE
(055) 239.65.05

FAX
None

TELEX
None

NUMBER OF ROOMS
4; all w/BST

CREDIT CARDS
None; cash only

RATES
1 or 2 persons L40,000; L3,000 for each shower

Hotel Archibusieri ★★
Vicolo Marzio, 1 (Piazza del Pesce)

Hotel Archibusieri is in the same building as the handsome Hotel Hermitage (see page 42). To locate the Archibusieri, stand at the foot of the Ponte Vecchio bridge with your back to the River Arno, and look to your right across the Piazza del Pesce for the Hotel Hermitage sign. When you find the building, you won't be able to use the elevator, because it is for the Hermitage exclusively. However, the walk up is just two short flights, and the Archibusieri is all on one floor.

This seven-room roost used to be a dark and dingy desperation choice. No more, thanks to a total redecoration that turned it completely around. Now it has uniform whitewashed walls and polished bamboo furnishings on terra-cotta floors. The rooms are still small, and no shower curtains have been added to protect the bathrooms from being drenched. But the new management is extremely nice and determined to make a go of the new operation, so a stay here should be pleasant.

English Spoken: Yes

Facilities & Services: Bar, direct-dial phones

Nearest Tourist Attractions: Uffizi Gallery, Ponte Vecchio, Arno, shopping

AREA
Ponte Vecchio

TELEPHONE
(055) 282.480 or 288.009

FAX
(055) 219.367

TELEX
None

NUMBER OF ROOMS
7; w/BST, 5; w/o BST, 2

CREDIT CARDS
MC, V

RATES
Single L70,000; double L95,000; triple L135,000; breakfast L10,000 extra

Hotel Hermitage ★★★
Vicolo Marzio, 1 (Piazza del Pesce)

AREA
Ponte Vecchio

TELEPHONE
(055) 287.216, 268.277, or
239.89.01

FAX
(055) 212.208

TELEX
None

NUMBER OF ROOMS
22; w/BST, 20; w/o BST, 2

CREDIT CARDS
MC, V

RATES
Single L110,000; double
L75,000–190,000; triple
L230,000; 20% discount
Nov 15–March 15; breakfast
included

One of my favorite hotels in Florence has always been the Hermitage, located on the top three floors of a building overlooking the Ponte Vecchio and the Arno. Recently it changed ownership and I worried that it would become slick and modern. I should not have wasted a nanosecond worrying, because after a well-deserved refurbishing, the results are smashing and the hotel is better than ever. Everything about this charming hotel is appealing, from the top-floor plant-filled terrace with its spectacular views, to the well-thought-out bedrooms and sitting areas. The cozy living room has a bar along one side and a fireplace for cool winter evenings. Oriental rugs are tossed on the tile floors, and yellow slipcovers add a touch of brightness to comfortable chairs and sofas that are perfect for sinking into and gazing out over the Arno. No two of the bedrooms are alike, but all are done with good taste and flair. They have muted wallpaper, a mixture of antique and reproduction furniture, and double-glazed windows to buffer the noise along the river. I especially like No. 1, with its lovely river view, large bathtub, and pretty hand-painted antique armoire. The management is professional and accommodating. To alleviate the impossible parking situation, they cooperate with a garage where you can leave your car while staying here. The hotel is so central to everything in Florence that a car would only be a nuisance.

English Spoken: Yes

Facilities & Services: Air-conditioning, bar, direct-dial phones, garage facilities L18,000–30,000 per day, hair dryers, lift

Nearest Tourist Attractions: Ponte Vecchio, Arno, central Florence

Hotel la Scaletta ★★
Via Guicciardini, 13

AREA
Ponte Vecchio

The hotel's guests are a convivial mixture of international travelers who know that obtaining a room here is no mean feat, but that their efforts will be amply rewarded. The hotel's draw is its near-perfect setting just over the Ponte Vecchio on Via Guicciardini, the street that leads to the Pitti Palace and Piazza Santo Spirito. With its wrinkled, cozy charm, you cannot expect anything modern or state-of-the-art, but you will have a warm welcome from the delightful owner, Barbara Barbieri, and her cat Micia, who moves from one warm spot to another throughout the day. Some rooms are huge, with marble fireplaces and high ceilings. Others are smaller but still roomy. They are furnished in assorted styles, with no plastic, Formica, or spindly metal in sight. Bathrooms are vintage but serviceable. There is a lift from the street to the hotel, which is on the second floor of an old palazzo near the American Express office. Once inside, the halls seem to go on forever, and there are numerous steps leading from one end of the rambling hotel to the other. A 360-degree view from the roof garden is nothing short of sensational. On a clear day, you can see all the way to Fiesole. Closer in, your view is of the Pitti Palace and the Boboli Gardens.

English Spoken: Yes

Facilities & Services: Bar, lift, meals on request, lockout at midnight

Nearest Tourist Attractions: Ponte Vecchio, Arno, Pitti Palace, Piazza Santo Spirito, shopping

Hotel Pensione Quisisana & Pontevecchio ★★★
Lungarno degli Archibusieri, 4

For those in search of a beautiful Florentine hotel, the Quisisana & Pontevecchio is the answer. The hotel is filled with character and history. Originally, the building was a stable for the Medici horses. In 1903, Signora Marasco's grandmother opened this wonderful hotel, which faces the Arno River. You will see her portrait hanging in the TV and card room. Today, everywhere you look, there is a pretty piece of furniture with a story attached, a bouquet of fresh or dried flowers, a nice painting, or an attractive print hanging on the wall. In the dining room, you

TELEPHONE
(055) 283.028 or 214.255

FAX
(055) 289.562

TELEX
None

NUMBER OF ROOMS
14; w/BST, 10; w/o BST, 4

CREDIT CARDS
MC, V

RATES
Single L55,000–70,000; double L85,000–110,000; triple L115,000–145,000; breakfast included

AREA
Ponte Vecchio

TELEPHONE
(055) 216.692 or 215.046

FAX
(055) 268.303

TELEX
None

NUMBER OF ROOMS
40; w/BST, 38; w/o BST, 2

CREDIT CARDS
AMEX, DC, MC, V

will sit on chairs that were made especially for the grand opening of the hotel at the turn of the century. In the hall outside the dining room, be sure to notice the chest, which is between 400 and 500 years old. It was used as a safe to hold pay for soldiers. To prevent theft, it was designed so that all of the locks on the chest must be open or closed at the same time. The hotel is proud of its devoted long-term staff, some of whom look as though they could have been on hand for the opening ceremonies.

As for the rooms, they have a dignified, lived-in look with the patina of age. Those facing the river have spectacular views. Scenes from E.M. Forster's *A Room with a View* were filmed in the loggia overlooking the Arno. Number 33, facing the river, has a lovely terrace where you can sit and watch the sun set over the Ponte Vecchio. The inlaid furniture is mostly antique, and so is the bathroom. As for the location, it has an A+ rating. You are right next to the Uffizi Gallery, minutes from the Ponte Vecchio and good shopping, and a ten-minute stroll to Il Duomo.

English Spoken: Yes

Facilities & Services: Bar, direct-dial phones, some hair dryers, lift

Nearest Tourist Attractions: You are staying in one; others include the Ponte Vecchio, Uffizi Gallery, shopping, Il Duomo

SAN LORENZO CENTRAL MARKET

Hotel Bellettini ★★
Via de' Conti, 7

You have to know about this one, for chances are you would not discover it on your own. While very central to all the action in Florence, it is tucked away through a courtyard entrance near the Capelle Medicee by the San Lorenzo Central Market. For decades it was operated by two aged sisters. No more. Now owned by Sr. Icilio, a new page has been turned and the two stars have been polished to a new luster.

One of the best features is the bathrooms, which have stall showers *with* doors and plenty of absorbent towels on hand. There is a two-room suite for families, with a beautiful hand-painted dresser and bed. The bath for this has a separately enclosed toilet, something you never find in a two-star hotel in Florence and seldom in a three. Room No. 33 receives honorable mention for its painted floral designs on a pull-down desk and matching bedside tables. In the halls and other public areas you will see stained-glass windows, Florentine oils, and handsomely painted ceilings. An old mantel has an original papal insignia hanging over it and serves as the hotel's logo. Before you leave, be sure to take a peak at the kitchen to admire the original ceiling.

English Spoken: Yes

Facilities & Services: 10 rooms with air-conditioning L7,000 per day, direct-dial phones, 10 rooms with TV

Nearest Tourist Attractions: Central Market, Il Duomo

RATES
Single L76,000;
double L90,000–126,000;
triple L165,000; suite for 4
L220,000; breakfast included

Hotel Enza ★
Via San Zanobi, 45

Every day during my stay in Florence to do the research for this book and *Cheap Eats in Italy*, I walked by this hotel coming or going to my apartment just a few doors beyond it. I could not tell much, because it is up a flight of stairs from the street entrance. Finally I went in and met the owner, Eugenia Del Mazza, who for 12 years has been working to provide deliberately budget-priced rooms to shoestring travelers and students looking for low-cost places to stay. At a one-star no one can expect *Architectural Digest* interiors or designer fabrics. True, the rooms have wild wallpaper and spreads that do not match, but there are no holes or cigarette burns and it is certainly clean. Eugenia is friendly and helpful, and the location is good. From here you can walk to the Central Market, the Piazza SS. Annunziata, and the train station. Lots of good Cheap Eats are close at hand, and a bakery across the street sells delicious sandwiches, salads, and cool drinks.

English Spoken: Yes

AREA
San Lorenzo Central Market

TELEPHONE
(055) 490.990

FAX
None

TELEX
571654

NUMBER OF ROOMS
15; w/BST, 8; w/o BST, 7

CREDIT CARDS
None; must pay every 3 days, in advance

RATES
Single L40,000;
double L60,000–70,000;
triple L85,000–100,000;
quad L100,000–120,000;
breakfast L8,000 extra (not served in off seasons)

Facilities & Services: None

Nearest Tourist Attractions: Central Market, Piazza SS. Annunziata, Il Duomo, and Arno, about 20–30 minutes depending on how much you browse along the way

TRAIN STATION

Albergo Adua ★
Via Fiume, 20

AREA
Train Station

TELEPHONE
(055) 239.83.22

FAX
None

TELEX
None

NUMBER OF ROOMS
7; all w/BST

CREDIT CARDS
None

RATES
Single L50,000; double L80,000; triple L105,000; breakfast included

Adua Petri takes guests under her wing, offering hospitality and tips on everything from what to see and do to where to shop and get your hair done for the best prices. Her homey seven-room pensione is on the second floor, with no elevator. From here, however, walking to almost everything in Florence is easy. All of the rooms are nice, especially No. 1 with its beautiful hand-painted ceiling, corner fireplace, and almost-antique furniture. Other rooms have ceiling fans, blond modern furniture, and some street noise. If you are a light sleeper, earplugs might be a good idea. Breakfast is served family-style around a communal table in the kitchen. This is a great place to practice your language skills with other travelers and exchange money-saving tips on Florence.

English Spoken: No

Facilities & Services: None

Nearest Tourist Attractions: Train station; can walk to almost everything else

Albergo Anna ★
Via Faenza, 56

AREA
Train Station

TELEPHONE
(055) 287.506

FAX
None

TELEX
None

NUMBER OF ROOMS
11; w/BST, 6; w/o BST, 5

CREDIT CARDS
None

Anna Pianigiani serves breakfast to her guests each morning in her large kitchen, which opens onto a balcony ablaze with flowering geraniums. After sitting around the communal table for two or three mornings, you just become one of the family and happily melt into the whole scene. Anna and her husband have taken over running the hotel from her parents, who must be in their nineties by now. *Everyone* works here, and not much gets by them, including exceptions to their iron-clad midnight curfew. Nine of the rooms have balconies facing the street or a quiet garden, but the charm stops there. Practicality does not, however, because the rooms are very clean, with pretty tile floors, Formica furniture, and good beds. You can't call it luxurious, but then neither are the prices.

English Spoken: Yes

Facilities & Services: None

Nearest Tourist Attractions: Train station; can walk to almost everything

RATES
Single L48,000–55,000; double L68,000–85,000; triple L85,000–105,000; breakfast L9,000 extra

Albergo Marcella ★
Via Faenza, 58

Albergo Marcella is another bargain for Cheap Sleepers who want to be near the train station. Actually, the area is far superior to most station neighborhoods, despite the fact that it is overrun with hotels, pensiones, and rooms geared to every size of pocketbook. Maria Noto and her husband have been running their seven-room place for 20 years. They never have tried to make it more than a plain, no-frills Cheap Sleep. The rooms are freshly painted, the curtains are clean, and the hall facilities are perfectly acceptable. The top-floor rooms are sunny, with no gloomy interior views. If you land in No. 3, you will be in an enormous double with a nice balcony, but you will have to shower down the hall. There is a midnight lockout, but for most this will not be a problem because Florence has few hot night spots to tempt all-night revelry.

English Spoken: Yes

Facilities & Services: None; midnight lockout

Nearest Tourist Attractions: Can walk to every tourist attraction on this side of Arno, and most on other side if you are hearty

AREA
Train Station

TELEPHONE
(055) 213.232

FAX
None

TELEX
None

NUMBER OF ROOMS
7; w/BST, 1; w/o BST, 6

CREDIT CARDS
None

RATES
Single L35,000; double L50,000–55,000; triple L22,000 per person

Albergo Marini ★
Via Faenza, 56

Neat, clean, and uniform in its plainness, the Albergo Marini is short on charm, but very serviceable. The antiseptically clean rooms are swabbed daily by the owner's wife, who never seems to smile,

AREA
Train Station

TELEPHONE
(055) 284.824

and with the amount of work she does it is easy to see why. The rooms have blond college dormitory–style furnishings, some with good views and others with gloomy interior outlooks into a courtyard. There is a lockout from 12:40 A.M. until 7:00 A.M. Breakfast is an additional 10,000 lire per person. My advice to you is to skip it here and eat in any one of the neighboring *caffes*, where you will have a more authentic Italian experience, especially if you stand at the bar while downing your cappuccino and *cornetto* (croissant).

English Spoken: Very limited

Facilities & Services: None; second-floor walk-up

Nearest Tourist Attractions: Central Market; can walk to Il Duomo and Ponte Vecchio in under a half hour; lots to see along the way

Albergo Merlini ★
Via Faenza, 56

The building houses several pensiones, but for my sleeping lire, the family-owned Merlini is the best of the bunch. The 15-room third-floor walk-up has a homey atmosphere presided over by a typical Italian family who is happy to share their TV viewing time with guests.

The wide hallways are filled with pretty antique pieces and above-average paintings and prints. There is a sunny glassed-in terrace that doubles as a breakfast area during the summer season. Rooms are definitely a notch above the usual one-star standard, and the hall facilities are clean. Most of the rooms have at least one or two nice pieces of furniture and nonthreatening fabric mixes. There are some lapses, such as last year's calendar still hanging on one wall, but if you end up in a bright room with your own little balcony, you won't mind, will you?

English Spoken: Yes

Facilities & Services: None; 1 A.M. lockout

Nearest Tourist Attractions: Can walk to Central Market and Il Duomo, and/or take a bus from the train station to every major site in Florence

FAX
None

TELEX
None

NUMBER OF ROOMS
12; w/BST, 6; w/o BST, 6

CREDIT CARDS
None

RATES
Single L35,000–42,000;
double L50,000–60,000; triple
L67,000; quad L85,000;
showers L3,000; breakfast
L10,000 extra

AREA
Train Station

TELEPHONE
(055) 212.848

FAX
None

TELEX
None

NUMBER OF ROOMS
12; w/BST, 3; w/o BST, 9

CREDIT CARDS
None

RATES
Single L35,000;
double L50,000–60,000;
extra person L22,500;
breakfast L8,000 extra

Albergo Mia Cara ★
Via Faenza, 58

The hotel has been owned and operated for two decades by the Noto family. Their approach is friendly, but guests must toe the line when it comes to drip-dry laundry and room feasts, and they enforce the 2 A.M. lockout without exception. The large rooms are light, clean, and airy, with baths that do not have shower curtains or soap. Some of the rooms are better than others in this one-star second-floor site that is *never* empty. Those to avoid are the quads, where a few of the beds are no more than cots. From March through June, the hotel is host to many student groups. The rest of the year, it is home to backpackers and other shoestring travelers seeking a midtown budget place to sleep and nothing more. During the off seasons, breakfast can be deducted from the room rate, but during the high season from July until October, you must pay for it whether you eat it or not.

English Spoken: Yes

Facilities & Services: None; lockout at 2 A.M.

Nearest Tourist Attractions: Train station; can walk to everything on this side of Arno (hearty souls will walk everywhere)

AREA
Train Station

TELEPHONE
(055) 216.053

FAX
(055) 230.2601

TELEX
None

NUMBER OF ROOMS
24; w/BST, 9; w/o BST, 15

CREDIT CARDS
None

RATES
Single L35,000–42,000; double L48,000–65,000; triple, add 35% of double price; breakfast L7,000 extra, except during high seasons, when it is added and cannot be deducted

Hotel Azzi ★
Via Faenza, 51

For five decades this 13-room hotel in a former monastery was presided over by the Azzi sisters. They recently retired and sold it to Alessandro Berti, a hopeful jazz musician. If all of his dreams and plans for change come true, he will have a unique Florence hotel. His idea is to create an artistic haven where struggling artists, poets, and musicians can stay, exchanging ideas and offering moral support to one another. Each room will be dedicated to a specific artist, and copies of their works will be displayed. I wish Alessandro *buon fortuna!*

For the time being, until he saves enough money and gets through the morass of Italian red tape

AREA
Train Station

TELEPHONE
(055) 213.806

FAX
(055) 213.806

TELEX
None

NUMBER OF ROOMS
13; all w/o BST

CREDIT CARDS
MC, V

RATES
Single L40,000; double L60,000; extra person L26,000; breakfast included

required to make any changes in any building, the hotel remains almost the same as it has for the last 56 years. This is not, however, to suggest that it is undesirable, because it isn't. The rooms are quiet and clean, with antiques tossed in here and there. A sunny terrace and a lovely dining room provide nice places for breakfast, which is complemented by assorted teas, cheeses, and meats in addition to the usual jam, butter, and rolls served with strong coffee. In the sitting room, a huge bookcase holds novels and art books in several languages for guests to borrow during their stay.

English Spoken: Yes

Facilities & Services: None

Nearest Tourist Attractions: Train station; can walk to almost everything

Hotel Lombardi ★★
Via Fiume, 8

AREA
Train Station

TELEPHONE
(055) 283.151

FAX
(055) 284.808

TELEX
None

NUMBER OF ROOMS
15; all w/BST

CREDIT CARDS
MC, V

RATES
Single L84,000; double L120,000; extra person 35% extra; breakfast included

The Lombardi is perfectly positioned if you want to be in sight of the railroad station and the convention center. The two-star family-owned and -run hotel has been redone in a simple modern style reminiscent of a Motel 6. There is no public sitting area, but the wide white-tiled halls have sofas and chairs where you can sit if you want to. Breakfast is served in a sunny room with a fully stocked bar to one side. The bedrooms lack any style, but they are spotlessly maintained and serviceable. After all, you are here to see Florence, not spend your time in a hotel room. The baths are fine. The showers have folding doors, but you must contend with limp cotton towels. The hotel belongs to the Family Hotel and Restaurant Group in Italy, and this means you will receive a warm and cordial welcome from your hostess, Rita Lombardi.

English Spoken: Yes

Facilities & Services: Bar, direct-dial phones, lift, TVs

Nearest Tourist Attractions: Il Duomo, Central Market within walking distance

Hotel Mario's ★★★
Via Faenza, 89

Mario Noce is the president of an independent group of family-owned hotels and restaurants in Italy. Naturally he is very well thought of in Florentine hotel circles, because his hotel reflects the very best in quality, value, and comfort, the goals the organization promotes. His hotel has been completely redone, using pieces from a beautiful collection of 16th-century antiques both in the public areas and in the 16 bedrooms. Mario's warmth and hospitality are evident at every turn, from the welcome in four languages at the reception desk to the bowls of fresh fruit in each room. Guests are encouraged to mingle and get to know one another at the bar in the early evening, or while seated at the communal breakfast tables in the morning. While you may find rooms in Florence for less, you will not be able to top Mario's for general ambience, friendliness, and a feeling of well-being.

English Spoken: Yes

Facilities & Services: Air-conditioning, bar, direct-dial phones, hair dryers, TVs

Nearest Tourist Attractions: Central Market with hundreds of stalls selling everything (meat, fish, poultry, vegetables, and fruit) inside, and leather, clothing, scarves, etc., outside; can walk to Il Duomo in less than 20 minutes

AREA
Train Station
TELEPHONE
(055) 216.801
FAX
(055) 212.039
TELEX
None
NUMBER OF ROOMS
16; w/BST, 15; w/o BST, 1
CREDIT CARDS
AMEX, DC, MC, V
RATES
Single L85,000–120,000; double L100,000–150,000; triple L150,000–220,000; discounts in off seasons; breakfast included

Hotel Nazionale ★
Via Nazionale, 22

Although not luxurious by any stretch of the imagination, Marie-Claude Hanotel's one-star hotel is a clean accommodation close to the railroad station. French-born and delightful, Marie-Claude runs the place along with the help of her friendly dog Figaro. The rooms are pleasing to the eye, with fresh whitewashed walls, royal blue carpets in some, and plain but scratch-free furniture. The rooms along the frantically busy Via Nazionale are noisy, but the windows are double-glazed to help quell the noise.

AREA
Train Station
TELEPHONE
(055) 238.22.03 or 262.203
FAX
None
TELEX
None
NUMBER OF ROOMS
9; w/BST, 5; w/o BST, 4
CREDIT CARDS
MC, V

RATES
Single L50,000–62,000;
double L77,000–88,000; triple
L118,000; discounts in winter;
breakfast included

Of course, if you open them, you won't have any soundproofing. For better sleeping prospects, request a quiet room on the back with a sunny exposure. The hotel is on the second floor on the right side of a gloomy building. Don't be put off by the drab approach or the dismal stairway leading to the hotel. Believe me, this one is a sure thing.

English Spoken: Yes

Facilities & Services: None

Nearest Tourist Attractions: Can walk to almost everything

Hotel Nuova Italia ★★
Via Faenza, 26

AREA
Train Station
TELEPHONE
(055) 287.508 or 268.430
FAX
(055) 210.941
TELEX
None
NUMBER OF ROOMS
21; all w/BST
CREDIT CARDS
AMEX, MC, V
RATES
Single L70,000; double
L110,000; triple L150,000;
quad L190,000; breakfast
included

Via Faenza is loaded with pensiones and family hotels of every type and description. The majority are small, dark, dingy, and—yes—cheap enough. But in the bargain you can forget about cleanliness and comfort. You will find none of this at the two-star Nuova Italia, owned by the Viti family, where pride of ownership is evident from the reception desk onward.

A lovely stone stairway with an iron rail leads guests to the rooms, which are uniformly carpeted and done in easy-care laminated wood furniture. A few rooms have screens (a rarity) to separate you and the hordes of mosquitos that live in Florence during the warm weather. Trust me, you *definitely* want one of these rooms unless you want to spend the night chasing that one last elusive mosquito around the room. A downstairs sitting room showcases the family collection of Italian watercolors. This is also where you will be served a Continental breakfast in the morning. The hotel is close to good restaurants (see *Cheap Eats in Italy*), interesting shopping (see "Cheap Chic," page 159), and most of the places visitors want to see in Florence.

English Spoken: Yes

Facilities & Services: Direct-dial phones

Nearest Tourist Attractions: Can walk to major sites

Hotel Palazzo Benci ★★★
Via Faenza, 6

The Hotel Palazzo Benci is in the renovated 16th-century mansion of the Benci family of Florence. This attractive uptown hotel is now owned and operated by the Braccia family. The service by family members and their staff is cordial and discreet. The compact, well-decorated rooms could be found in any major hotel around the world. They provide guests with all the creature comforts and are quiet, soothing oases after a sightseeing or shopping stint. The enclosed, flower-filled garden has tables with umbrellas for summer al fresco breakfasts or afternoon drinks. The ornate upstairs sitting room, with its gray and white marble floor and handsome, heavily scrolled ceilings, was a guest room in the original mansion. The tranquil rooms along the back overlook the Medici Chapel. All the rooms in the hotel have double-glazed windows and air-conditioning, so you will not be plagued with noise at any time, or swarms of mosquitos in the summer—if you remember to keep the windows closed.

English Spoken: Yes

Facilities & Services: Air-conditioning, bar, direct-dial phones, lift, mini-bars, room service for drinks or breakfast, TVs

Nearest Tourist Attractions: Central Market, Il Duomo, and all other tourist sites in Florence

AREA
Train Station

TELEPHONE
(055) 217.049, 262.821, or 213.848

FAX
(055) 288.308

TELEX
575851 PALBEN

NUMBER OF ROOMS
26; all w/BST

CREDIT CARDS
AMEX, DC, MC, V

RATES
Single L120,000; double L180,000; triple L240,000; off seasons, deduct L20,000; breakfast included

Hotel Pensione Tony's Inn ★ & Apollo ★★
Via Faenza, 77

Hotel Pensione Tony's Inn and the Apollo, operated under the ownership of Rose Zarb and her husband, Antonio Lelli, appeal to a wide student audience. Antonio is a photographer, and his interesting Tuscan portraits are framed and displayed throughout both hotels, where the mix of rooms is clean but the views are unimpressive. At Tony's, No. 7 has modern nondescript furniture, two hard chairs, a desk, and an armoire. Number 8 is a better double,

AREA
Train Station

TELEPHONE
(055) 284.119 or 217.975

FAX
(055) 210101

TELEX
None

NUMBER OF ROOMS
23; all w/BST

with a Florentine painted bed and wardrobe, a tile bath, and a chair in need of recovering. At the second-floor Apollo, the rooms are decidedly better. Most are sunny, with modern furniture, nice cotton bedspreads, and good baths. Rules for all guests are posted in both English and Japanese: They state that guests may not have visitors, do laundry, use any electrical appliances, or stay out past the 1:30 A.M. lockout. Both hotels are closed every year from November through February.

English Spoken: Yes

Facilities & Services: None

Nearest Tourist Attractions: Train station; almost everything within walking distance

Pensione Accademia ★
Via Faenza, 7

The Accademia has 16 rooms on three floors in a building on the hotel-studded Via Faenza. This area is known as hotel heaven, because no matter what your price range or level of tolerance for nightly digs, here you will have several choices. This hotel is nothing red-hot, but it is clean, safe, and family-run, and the prices will not leave you breathless. The original stained-glass windows from 1700 and a painted ceiling create a dramatic entry area. The breakfast room has another frescoed ceiling, a huge gilt mirror, and framed photos of Florence mixed with watercolors of Tuscany. Some rooms are better than others. The best are without a shower or toilet, having only a basin and a bidet. Several that do have showers have just a portable unit stuck in one corner of the bedroom, with the toilet down the hall. These rooms should be avoided at all costs. It is better to go on a real economy kick by reserving a room with only a sink and bidet and use the well-ventilated hall facilities.

English Spoken: Some

Facilities & Services: None

Nearest Tourist Attractions: Il Duomo, heart of Florence within 10-minute walk

---

CREDIT CARDS
MC, V

RATES
Tony's: Single L70,000; double L110,000; triple L140,000; quad L175,000. Apollo: Single L85,000; double L125,000; triple L165,000; quad L200,000. Breakfast included at both

AREA
Train Station

TELEPHONE
(055) 293.451

FAX
None

TELEX
None

NUMBER OF ROOMS
16; w/BST, 6; w/o BST, 10

CREDIT CARDS
AMEX, MC, V

RATES
Single L40,000–50,000; double L55,000–68,000; extra person add 35%; breakfast L12,000 extra

Pensione Ausonia ★
Via Nazionale, 24

The back rooms are best here if uninterrupted sleep is a priority. Otherwise, the rooms on the front facing the traffic-choked Via Nazionale will be reminiscent of a pit stop at the Indianapolis 500 speedway. The plain rooms are not intended for long, leisurely stays, but for a two- or three-night Cheap Sleep in Florence, they will certainly do. You can save even more lire if you do not take the breakfast at 8,000 lire, but go to a neighborhood *caffè* and eat for about one third of this amount. The location is within walking distance to the major sites, the colorful central market, the train station, and loads of good restaurants (see *Cheap Eats in Italy*). An added bonus is a 5 percent discount given to readers who present a copy of *Cheap Sleeps in Italy* when reserving and checking in.

English Spoken: Yes
Facilities & Services: Lift
Nearest Tourist Attractions: Train station; major sites within walking distance

AREA
Train Station
TELEPHONE
(055) 496.547
FAX
(055) 496324
TELEX
None
NUMBER OF ROOMS
11; w/BST, 6; w/o BST, 5
CREDIT CARDS
AMEX, MC, V
RATES
Single L40,000–50,000; double L55,000–70,000; L22,000 each additional person in room; 5% discount for readers of *Cheap Sleeps in Italy*; breakfast L8,000 extra

Pensione Daniel (no stars)
Via Nazionale, 22

Trying to get advance reservations at the Pensione Daniel is about as easy as securing a papal audience at the last minute if you are a Methodist. If you want to stay here, you will have to show up early in the day and hope for the best, because this Cheap Sleeping thrill is internationally known as one of the lowest-cost beds in Florence. Never mind that the owner needs a crash course at Dale Carnegie; that showers are extra and available *only* between 7 and 9:30 A.M.; that there is a rigid midnight lockout; and that to get to this third-floor site, you must hike up 72 long and steep steps. The well-worn rooms are perfect for those whose love of a Cheap Sleep, come hell or high water, surpasses their desire for much comfort. On a more positive note, the rooms are repainted almost every year in bright pink, yellow, and blue Easter egg colors, and the location is within walking distance of the

AREA
Train Station
TELEPHONE
(055) 211.293
FAX
None
TELEX
None
NUMBER OF ROOMS
4; w/BST, none; w/o BST, all. There is only one public bathroom
CREDIT CARDS
None; cash only
RATES
1 or 2 persons L30,000; L15,000 each extra person

train station, the big Central Market with all its alluring stalls, Il Duomo, and the Ponte Vecchio.

English Spoken: No

Facilities & Services: None

Nearest Tourist Attractions: Train station; central Florence within walking distance

VIA TORNABUONI

Hotel Tornabuoni Beacci ★★★
Via Tornabuoni, 3

AREA
Via Tornabuoni

TELEPHONE
(055) 212.645, 268.377, or 294.283

FAX
(055) 283.594

TELEX
None

NUMBER OF ROOMS
30; all w/BST

CREDIT CARDS
AMEX, DC, MC, V

RATES
Single L130,000; double L250,000; during July and Aug, half-board not required; full-board an additional L25,000 per person per meal; breakfast included in all rates. *Note:* All prices include half-board, an additional L25,000 per person per meal (lunch and/or dinner)

Comments such as "Just what we have been looking for," "It is nice to feel at home so far away from home," and "Good food!" are only a few of those· written by enthusiastic visitors in the guest book, which dates back to 1917 when Signora Beacci's parents began this delightful Florentine hotel. Over the years, the devoted clientele of writers, actors, models, and just plain tourists have returned time and again, largely because of the warm personality of Signora Beacci and the way she makes everyone feel right at home. Everything about the hotel, which is on the third and fourth floors of an old palazzo in the heart of Florence, is gracious and discerning without being pretentious. The sitting room with its wood-burning fireplace is comfortable and classically furnished with antiques, big sofas, and easy chairs, and with lovely tapestries hanging on the walls. The bedrooms are done in pastels, with painted furniture mixed with vintage wood. These rooms are so inviting that you may want to settle in and stay forever. A wisteria-shaded rooftop terrace for afternoon drinks or a leisurely breakfast offers splendid views of the nearby churches and red-tiled roofs. Guests have a choice of eating three meals a day at the hotel, or just breakfast and one other. In July and August, half-board is not required, but at the price, believe me it is a steal when you compare the food, service, and ambience to what you would get elsewhere for the same price.

English Spoken: Yes

Facilities & Services: Air-conditioning, bar, direct-dial phones, mini-bars, restaurant, room service, TVs

Nearest Tourist Attractions: Central Florence, Il Duomo, and premier shopping

La Residenza ★★★
Via Tornabuoni, 8

La Residenza is a throwback to the past, when people came to study and enjoy the art and architecture of Florence for an entire "season." In those days, one checked into a favorite pensione, where breakfast and at least one other meal was served. Today it is almost impossible to find such a pensione in Florence. Welcome to La Residenza. From May through October, guests are required to take half-board (breakfast and dinner), but during the rest of the year, it is optional.

The pensione, owned by Giovanna Vasileo and her husband for the past 17 years, occupies the top four floors of a 16th-century Renaissance palace right next to the Palazzo Strozzi. To get to the reception desk, you will ride up from the ground floor in one of the first elevators in Florence. Yes, things need some paint, and there is a little wear and tear around the edges, but this does not take away from Signora Vasileo's graciousness or the at-home feeling one has while staying here. The sitting rooms are filled with her own antiques and blue velvet–covered chairs and couches. The welcoming dining room is set with linens, nice china, and polished glassware. Fresh flowers add a lovely touch. No two of the bedrooms are alike, and there is no denying their "old slipper" appeal. Most have high ceilings, large windows, and a mix of furniture. The bathrooms are mostly small, with tiny showers. The best havens are on the top floors, with their own plant-filled terraces.

English Spoken: Yes

Facilities & Services: Air-conditioning (L3,500 per person per day), bar, direct-dial phones, hair dryers, lift, restaurant, room service, some TVs

Nearest Tourist Attractions: Best fashion and boutique shopping, Palazzo Strozzi, Arno, Il Duomo

AREA
Via Tornabuoni

TELEPHONE
(055) 284.197

FAX
(055) 284.197

TELEX
None

NUMBER OF ROOMS
24; all w/BST

CREDIT CARDS
AMEX, DC, MC, V

RATES
With half-board:
Single L150,000; double L130,000 per person; triple L125,000 per person.
No board (off seasons only):
Single L90,000; double L130,000 for 2; triple L175,000. Breakfast included all year

Soggiorno Cestelli ★
Borgo SS. Apostoli, 25

AREA
Uffizi Gallery

TELEPHONE
(055) 314.213

FAX
None

TELEX
None

NUMBER OF ROOMS
7; w/BST, 1; w/o BST, 6

CREDIT CARDS
None

RATES
Single L45,000; double L70,000–85,000; breakfast included

Although it is hidden away, this hotel is well located for all the main sights in Florence. For a one-star on a narrow street in the heart of the old city, the Soggiorno Cestelli is nothing short of unbelievable. The approach, up two flights of stairs, is not inspiring. But once you have reached the small entrance hall and spotted the family antiques, you will know you have arrived at a special place. In 1934, Ada Cestelli's mother opened the door of their seven-room home to paying guests. Since that time, a loyal following has developed, making reservations, secured with an Italian lire deposit, essential months in advance. As you look around, you will see wonderful touches everywhere: pretty tassels holding back heavy curtains, tables displaying small collectibles, a pretty chair here, a nice painting or print there. Room No. 2 is amazing. It is a huge room with a massive armoire, bed, and matching bureau. A picture of the Madonna hangs over the bed. An ornate coatrack sits in one corner, and a gold standing mirror occupies another. The bidet and sink are screened off from the rest of the room, which is large enough to accommodate a sofa and chair in addition to everything else. Breakfast served in bed is available to those in the double room, but if you are alone, you will be served in the tiny dining room with the kitchen to one side.

English Spoken: Yes

Facilities & Services: None

Nearest Tourist Attractions: Uffizi Gallery, Arno, easy walk to Il Duomo and excellent shopping

OTHER OPTIONS

CAMPING

For the rough and ready, camping can provide some unusually Cheap Sleeps. Most sites are open all year, but are at least 30 minutes by bus from Florence proper. You can rent almost everything you need, and the sites available range from those that will accommodate a motorcycle and a tent to those big enough for a car and trailer. The prices quoted are per person and include water and electricity hookup. There is usually a small convenience store on the premises, but due to the captive audience, prices can be high.

Camping Panoramico
Via Peramonda, 1

> **Area:** Outside of Florence
> **Telephone:** (055) 599.069
> **Fax:** None
> **Telex:** None
> **Credit Cards:** AMEX, MC, V
> **Rates:** Open all year; L8,000 per person in camper or tent; L13,900 for car and trailer or camper; L7,000 for tent
> **English Spoken:** Yes
> **Facilities & Services:** Store and bar open in summer; showers included
> **Nearest Tourist Attractions:** None; 20–30 minutes to Florence by bus

Italiani e Stranieri
Viale Michelangelo, 80

> **Area:** Outside of Florence
> **Telephone:** (055) 681.19.77
> **Fax:** None
> **Telex:** None
> **Credit Cards:** None
> **Rates:** Open April–Oct 6 A.M.–midnight; L6,000 per person; L7,000 for tent; L12,000 for car and van; L4,000 for car only
> **English Spoken:** Yes
> **Facilities & Services:** Bar, market, showers included
> **Nearest Tourist Attractions:** About 20 minutes from Florence; beautiful views, but very crowded

Villa Camerata
Viale Augusto Righi 2A

Area: Outside Florence
Telephone: (055) 610.300
Fax: None
Telex: None
Credit Cards: None
Rates: Open all year; L5,000–9,000 for tents; L9,000 for car and tent
English Spoken: Yes
Facilities & Services: Showers included; affiliated with International Youth Hostel (see page 115); bar serving dinner only, from 6 P.M.
Nearest Tourist Attractions: None; must use public transportation to get to Florence

RESIDENCE HOTELS AND APARTMENTS

If you plan to be in Florence for longer than a week, a good way to cut costs is to stay in an apartment or a residence hotel. Most of the residence hotels are of at least three-star quality and provide all the services and amenities found in good hotels. Other advantages include more space and comfort, a kitchen where you can cook a few meals and save on restaurant costs, and the feeling of being more at home than you would be in a hotel room.

International Services Apartment Rentals

See Rome, page 110.

Residence Palazzo Ricasoli
Via delle Mantellate, 2

AREA
Piazza delle Libertà
TELEPHONE
(055) 352.151
FAX
(055) 495.001
TELEX
574504 Repari

In 1538, Bishop Giovan Battista Ricasoli commissioned architect Cosimo Bartolo to design this palace. Then, by order of Cosimo de' Medici, it became a monastery, with gardens that extended to the city walls. Today the gardens are gone, but the palazzo is a lovely residence hotel offering accommodations from studios to three-room apartments to those who are lucky enough to be able to stay longer in Florence.

The decor is modern, and the kitchens are fully equipped. In addition, a rooftop solarium, a tennis court, a conference room, and secretarial services are available. The longer the stay, the better the price discount. If you have a car, the location is ideal because it is just off the Florence ring road, and there is plenty of parking. From a tourist's point of view, it is quite a way from the city center, but the upscale residential area is interesting. Within only a few blocks of the Residence are shops and stalls selling everything you need to set up housekeeping, so you will get a real glimpse of day-to-day life in Florence. And in about a 15- or 20-minute walk, you will be at the wonderful central market, which has everything you have ever needed or wanted, and more.

English Spoken: Yes

Facilities & Services: Air-conditioning, bar, direct-dial phones, lift, fully equipped kitchens, parking L12,000 per day, TVs, maid service

Nearest Tourist Attractions: None; must walk about 25 minutes or use public transportation

NUMBER OF ROOMS
100; all w/BST

CREDIT CARDS
AMEX, DC, MC, V

RATES
Studios start at L100,000 per night; 2-room apartments start at L175,000; 3-room apartments start at L245,000; breakfast served only to groups by prior arrangement

Residence Porta al Prato
Via Ponte alle Mosse, 16

Renting your own vacation apartment anywhere in Italy can become an expensive burlesque. Italy is a land not only of lovely villas, but of near-impossible landlords and rental agents and Byzantine laws. To eliminate the ulcer-producing aggravation and supreme frustration that are guaranteed to be part of a do-it-yourself package, make reservations at a residence hotel. The prices may appear high at first, but remember: You are getting lots of space in a fully equipped, clean apartment where everything works, or will in short order. Of course, the longer you stay, the better the discount.

In Florence, the Residence Porte al Prato is an attractive choice. Each unit has standardized modern furniture, good closets, spacious bathrooms, a free parking slot, and maid service. The street in front is noisy most of the time, so be sure to request a balcony

AREA
Piazzale di Porta al Prato

TELEPHONE
(055) 354.951

FAX
(055) 354.956

TELEX
None

NUMBER OF ROOMS
46 apartments; all w/BST

CREDIT CARDS
None; cash only

RATES
Studios start at L110,000; 2-bedded apartments start at L140,000; 3-bedded apartments start at L180,000

room on the back. From a tourist's perspective, the location is about a 20-minute walk to action central.

English Spoken: Yes

Facilities & Services: Air-conditioning, direct-dial phones, lift, free parking, TV extra

Nearest Tourist Attractions: None; must walk or use nearby public transportation

STUDENT ACCOMMODATIONS

Student accommodations vary widely, from rooms for two or three to dorms housing up to 20 sleepers a night. Most of the sites impose a lockout during the day (i.e., you cannot stay in your room during this period) and a curfew at night. There is nothing elaborate about any of them; they are strictly places to lay a weary head. If possible, try to look at the room before you decide to stay there. Another point to remember is that often these accommodations are far from the city, entailing long bus commutes. It could be cheaper in the long run to find a small pensione closer in and apply the bus fares to the room rates.

Istituto Artigianelli Pensionato Pio X
Via de' Serragli, 106

AREA
Piazza Santo Spirito

TELEPHONE
(055) 225.044

FAX
None

TELEX
None

NUMBER OF ROOMS
16; w/BST, 3; w/o BST, 13

CREDIT CARDS
None

RATES
Single L20,000; double L35,000–45,000; triple L20,000 per person; breakfast L6,000 extra

The quiet location and the policies of no daytime lockout and no more than five persons to a room make this an attractive hostel choice. Originally the building was a convent, with two schools and a marble workshop. For the last 25 years it has been a hostel appealing to groups and/or individuals needing mighty Cheap Sleeps. The dormitory rooms are bare-bones basic, with thin mattresses on army-style cots. Up to ten people share the hall toilets and baths. There are no kitchen privileges, but you can bring in food and eat it in the dining room. There is a five-night maximum stay and a midnight curfew. The management is friendly, and there are no draconian rules posted all over the place.

English Spoken: Yes

Facilities & Services: None

Nearest Tourist Attractions: Piazza Santo Spirito, Pitti Palace

Ostello della Gioventù Europa Villa Camerata
Viale Augusto Righi, 2–4

The Villa Camerata is affiliated with the International Federation of Youth Hostels, so your card will be good here. Although it is northeast of Florence and requires at least a 30-minute bus ride to get into the city, the hostel is a popular choice due to its setting in a magnificent villa surrounded by lovely gardens. There are 400 beds and a three-day limit. Breakfast, sheets, and showers are included, but dinner is extra. It is important to know that there are *very* few places to eat nearby, so you must either eat in Florence or opt for the dinner served here. There is an 11:30 P.M. curfew and a daytime lockout from 9 A.M. to 2 P.M., when everyone must be out of his or her room. The reception desk is open from 9 A.M. to 1 P.M. and 3 P.M. to 7 P.M. Monday through Friday. However, before going all the way out here, be sure to call to see if these hours have changed, which they frequently do. Reservations are preferred in advance by mail.

> **English Spoken:** Enough
> **Facilities & Services:** None
> **Nearest Tourist Attractions:** None

AREA
Outside of Florence

TELEPHONE
(055) 601.451

FAX
(055) 600.315

TELEX
None

NUMBER OF ROOMS
400 beds; w/BST, none; w/o BST, all

CREDIT CARDS
None

RATES
L18,000 per person, single or in groups; dinner L12,000 per person; breakfast included

Santa Monaca Hostel
Via Santa Monaca, 6

Santa Monaca Hostel is across the river from Florence. It is popular, spacious, and clean, and it offers kitchen privileges, a safe for valuables, and a list of rules set in concrete. Each morning a loudspeaker booms music into the rooms at 8 A.M. to be sure everyone is awake. You must be out of your room *for the day* from 9:30 A.M. to 4 P.M. Lights are turned out at 11:30 P.M., and the door is locked at midnight. No reservations for individuals are taken; however, for groups of 15 or more, advance reservations are accepted. Individuals must show up between 9:30 A.M. and 1 P.M., when a sign-up sheet with vacancies is posted. You will have to return between 4 and 5:30

AREA
Piazza Santo Spirito

TELEPHONE
(055) 268.338 or 296.704

FAX
None

TELEX
None

NUMBER OF ROOMS
35; w/BST, none; w/o BST, all

CREDIT CARDS
None

RATES
L15,000 per night, 7-night maximum; L2,500 for sheets; breakfast L3,800–4,800 extra; lunch L14,000 extra

to claim your reservation and pay for it, or it will be cancelled. Accommodations are in large rooms with bunk beds sleeping 6 to 20 per room. A dining room is open for breakfast and lunch.

English Spoken: Enough

Facilities & Services: None

Nearest Tourist Attractions: Piazza Santo Spirito, Pitti Palace

ROME

Everyone sooner or later comes by Rome.
                                   —Robert Browning, 1868

The Romans take their city for granted. They are used to sipping espressos or cool drinks in a sidewalk *caffè* next to a piazza used by gladiators centuries ago. Ruined temples, triumphal arches, and Baroque fountains are every place, yet this vibrant city of over three million people refuses to be just a museum of history, art, and legend. The historic center includes the seven hills of the ancient walled city and contains 300 palaces, 280 churches, the ruins of imperial Rome, numerous parks and gardens, the residence of the Italian president, the houses of parliament, and government offices as well as banks, businesses, hotels, shops, and restaurants. Yes, it is crowded and the traffic jams are legion, with distances gauged by centimeters, not kilometers. Julius Caesar banned traffic during daylight, and in parts of Rome today, cars are banned both night and day. It is often faster, and always more interesting, to walk.

Rome was not built in a day, and it should not be visited in one. Rome can be like a good pizzeria: hot, noisy, smoke-filled, overflowing with people, and with more choices than you can handle. Take your time and allow it to grow on you gradually.

La dolce vita—yes, it exists, but it will cost you. There are *very few* inexpensive hotels in the center of Rome. Many that did exist a few years ago have upgraded and crossed over the line to moderate and expensive. Unless you are willing to live very, very simply, plan on spending at least $80 to $90 per night, and more realistically about $125 to $150, for a decent double in a well-located hotel. Even though the city is large, most of the hotels in *Cheap Sleeps in Italy* are within easy walking distance of the best sightseeing, dining, and shopping destinations.

The hotel prices depend on the type of hotel, the season, the location of the room, and perhaps its size. Government ratings do not depend on decoration, the grandeur of the building, or the attitude of the owner; they depend only on the facilities offered. Never judge a hotel by its stars, because some one-stars in Rome offer more value than many three-stars, which can be cold, ugly, and impersonal, never mind expensive.

The best-priced hotel rooms always fill up fast, therefore it is important to reserve your room in advance. Prices vary with the time of year, but it always pays to try to bargain down a rate. The willingness of management to bargain increases with the length of your stay, the number of vacancies, and the size of your party.

Avoid like the plague the "official" looking "tour operators" who lurk around the railroad station offering to find you a room. You will be directed to a sleazy dump with cigarette burns on the bedspreads and dirty toilets, at a price that is way too high for what you are getting.

If you are looking for a wild time in Rome, institutional accommodations are not the way to go. Religious institutions, convents, and monasteries welcome boarders of all faiths in the summer, but their strict curfews will put a damper on frivolity after 11 P.M., just when the nightlife is warming up.

USEFUL INFORMATION

Emergencies:	
Police, fire, ambulance	113
Medical assistance	International Medical Center, Via Amendola, 7; English spoken; doctors on call 24 hours a day; will send doctor to hotel; 462.371
English-speaking doctors	Salvator Mundi International Hospital, Viale Mura Gianicolensi, 67; 586.041
Tourist first aid	462.371
24-hour pharmacy	Carlo Erva, Via del Corso, 125; 679.08.66; Farmacia Internazionale, Piazza Barberini, 49; 462.996
24-hour dentist	Istituto George Eastman, 44.53.228
American Embassy	Via Veneto, 121; 46.741; American Embassy Health Unit, 467.42.150/1
British Embassy	Venti Settembre, 80A; 475.54.41
Canadian Embassy	Via G.B. De Rossi, 27; 855.341
Banks	American Service Bank, Piazza Mignanelli, 5; 678.68.15; Chase Manhattan Bank, Via M. Mercati, 31; 844.361
Currency exchange	American Express, Piazza di Spagna (Spanish Steps), 38, Mon–Fri 9 A.M.–5:30 P.M., Sat 9 A.M.–1 P.M.; no commission for their traveler's checks;

	72.28.01; Corso Rinascimento, 73–75, Mon–Fri 9 A.M.–1 P.M. and 3–5:30 P.M., Sat 9 A.M.–1 P.M.; 654.84.06
Taxis	3875, 4994, 3570, 8433 Radio taxi; accepts American Express and Diners Card; specify which card you will be using; 3875
Time	161
Morning wake-up service	114
Postal information	160, 180
Telephone code for Rome	06

HOTELS IN ROME BY AREA

AVENTINE

Hotels S. Anselmo & Villa S. Pio ★★★
Piazza S. Anselmo, 2

Hotel Aventino ★★
Via S. Domenico, 10

Hotels S. Anselmo and Villa S. Pio
AREA
Aventine
TELEPHONE
(06) 574.51.74, 578.32.14, or 574.52.31/2
FAX
(06) 578.36.04
TELEX
622812 SELMO I
NUMBER OF ROOMS
65; all w/BST
CREDIT CARDS
AMEX, MC, V
RATES
Single L135,000; double L195,000; triple L240,000; lower group and off-season rates; breakfast included

Hotel Aventino
AREA
Aventine
TELEPHONE
(06) 574.51.74 or 578.32.14
FAX
(06) 578.36.04
TELEX
622812 SELMO I
NUMBER OF ROOMS
23; all w/BST
CREDIT CARDS
AMEX, MC, V
RATES
Single L100,000; double L150,000; triple L195,000; breakfast included

Maria Luisa De Angelis's three hotels are in the Aventine district of Rome, a quiet, secluded residential area filled with lovely old villas. To stay in one of her hotels you will need sturdy walking shoes and a good set of lungs for the uphill climb from the bus stop about 20 minutes away, or be willing to use taxis or your own car to get into the center of Rome. While the hotels are definitely out of the mainstream, they are included for those pilgrims who seek a tranquil location set in lovely gardens, where they may wake to the sound of birds, not honking horns.

Of the three hotels, the elegant S. Anselmo is the best choice. The rooms are all beautifully decorated with hand-painted furniture, monogrammed sheets and pillow cases, and appliquéd cotton bedspreads. Many have magnificent terraces and dreamy bathrooms with tubs, separate stall showers, heated towel racks, and soft floral tile motifs. The downstairs sitting rooms and eating areas are furnished with an impressive collection of antiques and oil paintings, accented by bouquets of fresh flowers and potted plants.

The Aventino and Villa S. Pio are regrettably not up to par with the S. Anselmo. While the friendly welcome and services remain the same, some rooms are done in bleak modern furnishings that are a far cry from the spirit of these lovely old homes. The baths tend to be dated, and the narrow halls could use a fresh coat of paint. Unless a sudden transformation has taken place, or you are not too fussy about the looks of your surroundings, I recommend staying at the S. Anselmo if you decide on this location for your stay in Rome.

English Spoken: Yes

Facilities & Services: *Hotels S. Anselmo & Villa S. Pio:* Bar, direct-dial phones, some hair dryers, lift, some parking spaces (free), room service for light snacks, TVs (L10,000 extra), conference room. *Hotel Aventino:* Direct-dial phones, free parking spaces, TVs (L10,000 extra)

Nearest Tourist Attractions: None; must use bus, car, or taxi

Hotel Santa Prisca ★★
Largo Manlio Gelsomini, 25

You will find the quiet and dignified Santa Prisca Hotel in the Aventine residential district of Rome. This is definitely not a hub location, but many Rome veterans enjoy being out of the noisy, traffic-clogged city center in an area where they can experience more of the day-to-day life of Rome. This 1960s-style hotel is run by an order of Argentine nuns and offers 50 rooms, all with private baths, direct-dial telephones, and air-conditioning, which has just been added. Other drawing cards are the free parking and the restaurant, which serves three basic meals a day from a daily-changing menu. Even though the rooms are somewhat plain, they are immaculate. I also like the reading lights over the beds, the spacious closets, the pull-down desks, and the showers *with* curtains. For lazy afternoons soaking up the sun, there is a lovely garden. If you are not into hotel dining, the area is well known for its many fine restaurants.

English Spoken: Yes

Facilities & Services: Air-conditioning, bar, direct-dial phones, lift, free parking, restaurant (lunch and/ or dinner about L30,000 per person without beverage), TVs (L10,000 extra per day)

Nearest Tourist Attractions: Aventine, Baths of Caracalla

AREA
Aventine

TELEPHONE
(06) 574.19.17

FAX
None

TELEX
None

NUMBER OF ROOMS
50; all w/BST

CREDIT CARDS
MC, V

RATES
Single L115,000; double L135,000; triple L180,000; breakfast included

Albergo della Lunetta ★★
Piazza del Paradiso, 68

AREA
Campo de' Fiori
TELEPHONE
(06) 686.10.80 or 686.36.87
FAX
(06) 689.20.28
TELEX
None
NUMBER OF ROOMS
30; w/BST, 13; w/o BST, 17
CREDIT CARDS
None
RATES
Single L40,000–60,000;
double L70,000–90,000;
triple L90,000–120,000

Albergo della Lunetta consists of 30 functional rooms on four floors overlooking an interior courtyard. There is a pretty, plant-filled second-floor terrace and a comfortable lounge with brown Naugahyde sofas and chairs where guests gather to exchange travel tips. Some of the rooms are noisy. In a few the wallpaper could use some glue, and the triples are mighty scant on space. On the plus side, the hall facilities are perfectly adequate, so there is no need to pay extra for private ones unless you want to. For backpackers and other nondemanding guests of any age in search of sleeping accommodations with prices that don't burn holes in a budget, this one cannot be ignored. The stellar location places guests within walking distance of many good restaurants (see *Cheap Eats in Italy*) and the colorful daily outdoor market on Campo de' Fiori.

English Spoken: Limited
Facilities & Services: Direct-dial phones
Nearest Tourist Attractions: Campo de' Fiori, Piazza Navona

Albergo del Sole ★★
Via del Biscione, 76

AREA
Campo de' Fiori
TELEPHONE
(06) 654-0873, 678.94.46, or
654.52.58
FAX
(06) 689.37.87
TELEX
None
NUMBER OF ROOMS
62; w/BST, 30; w/o BST, 32
CREDIT CARDS
None
RATES
Single L55,000–70,000;
double L70,000–100,000; extra
person, add 35%

Albergo del Sole sits on the remains of the ancient Roman Pompeius Theater, which dates back to 55 B.C. It is the type of Cheap Sleep that appeals to those who do not mind a laid-back management approach and can overlook rough spots around the edges. Wide whitewashed halls that seem to go on forever display a collection of Roman posters, green plants, and a smattering of old furniture. There is an attractive outside patio with a fountain, and an inner courtyard with ancient paintings. The Art Nouveau dining room with two breakfronts and a large table is probably the nicest public room in the hotel, but it is never used because no meals are served. The bedrooms range from frankly rustic to adequate, especially those with private facilities. The showers are not American-inspired, by any means. Most are just a spout aimed at a wood-slat foot stand. Naturally, there are no curtains to keep the water from spraying everything. Think grade-school camp showers and you will get the picture perfectly.

English Spoken: Yes

Facilities & Services: Direct-dial phones, lift, parking (L20,000 per day)

Nearest Tourist Attractions: Campo de' Fiori, Piazza Navona

Albergo Pomezia ★★
Via dei Chiavari, 12

Clean and tidy rooms in a 50-year-old family-run hotel not too far from Piazza Navona and Campo de' Fiori describes the Pomezia. Under the stewardship of Maurizio Mariani, his brother, and their mother, the 22-room hotel reflects a pride of ownership all too lacking in many small Roman hotels today. The eight rooms on the first floor are newly redone, with coordinated colors, built-in wardrobes, luggage racks, and good bedside lighting. Seven are doubles with private facilities, and the one single has its bath and toilet in the hall, but no other room shares it, so it is quite private. In the older section, the rooms are rather characterless and a bit faded, but all pass the white-glove test for dust. Discounts in the off seasons make this budget nest even more appealing, and the reasonably priced Continental breakfast means you don't have to look elsewhere for your morning cappuccino and *cornetto*.

English Spoken: Yes

Facilities & Services: Bar for soft drinks and coffee, 8 rooms with direct-dial phones

Nearest Tourist Attractions: Campo de' Fiori, Piazza Navona, Piazza Venezia

AREA
Campo de' Fiori and Piazza Navona

TELEPHONE
(06) 686.13.71

FAX
None

TELEX
None

NUMBER OF ROOMS
22; w/BST, 10; w/o BST, 12

CREDIT CARDS
AMEX, MC, V

RATES
Single L50,000–80,000; double L80,000–100,000; triple L110,000–140,000; no charge for showers; discounts in off seasons; breakfast L3,000 downstairs, L5,000 in room

Hotel Arenula ★★
Via Santa Maria de' Calderari, 47

The Arenula is a find for the traveler who wants a reasonably priced hotel near the heart of old Rome,

AREA
Campo de' Fiori

TELEPHONE
(06) 689.61.88, 687.94.54, or
687.79.93
FAX
(06) 689.61.88
TELEX
None
NUMBER OF ROOMS
52; w/BST, 32; w/o BST, 20
(shower only)
CREDIT CARDS
MC, V
RATES
Single L70,000–85,000;
double L90,000–110,000;
triple, add 35%; breakfast
L8,000 extra

just across the Ponte Garibaldi from Trastevere. The no-nonsense, uniformly austere bedrooms have easy-wipe blond furnishings, white walls, tiled floors, and striped canvas bedspreads. Almost half come equipped with private bathrooms. The combination reception and lobby area is dominated by a big-screen television usually turned to a sporting event, probably to please the desk staff. To reach this hotel, you must first climb one flight of stairs to the first-floor lobby. Hopefully your room won't be three more flights up on the fourth floor. Nonathletically inclined Cheap Sleepers may want to think twice about this one if stairs are a problem.

English Spoken: Yes

Facilities & Services: Direct-dial phones, hair dryers, TVs

Nearest Tourist Attractions: Tiber, Trastevere, historic old Rome, Campo de' Fiori

Hotel Rinascimento ★★★
Via del Pellegrino, 122

AREA
Campo de' Fiori
TELEPHONE
(06) 687.48.13
FAX
(06) 683.35.18
TELEX
620207
NUMBER OF ROOMS
20; all w/BST
CREDIT CARDS
None
RATES
Single L109,000;
double L160,000; L65,000 for
extra person in room; breakfast
included

Location, location, location—that is the primary asset of the Rinascimento, a reliable bet for a simple, short stay in Rome. From the front door, you are five minutes away from the Piazza Navona, the Campo de' Fiori, the Piazza Farnese, and scores of good restaurants (see *Cheap Eats in Italy*). In about 15 minutes, you can walk to the Vatican or to the Pantheon. The building has a checkered past. It began its life in 1490 as a monastery, later became a classy brothel, and now houses this 20-room hotel. The rather spacious rooms and older-style bathrooms won't dazzle anyone, but they are acceptable and clean. The management is pleasant, but I wish they would post a nonsmoking sign for the desk staff.

English Spoken: Limited

Facilities & Services: Air-conditioning (L20,000 extra per day), bar, direct-dial phones, hair dryers, lift, mini-bars, TVs

Nearest Tourist Attractions: Piazza Navona, Campo de' Fiori, Pantheon

Hotel Smeraldo ★★
Vicolo dei Chiodaroli, 9

Spotless redecorated rooms in a pleasant atmosphere await guests at the Smeraldo. The rooms are not overdone, and extras such as comfortable chairs and television sets are not part of the bargain, but the paint is fresh and everything not only looks, but smells clean. The back views overlook a tiny courtyard, and the rooms along the front face an interesting old building across the street. Noise is at a minimum, so the windows can be kept open at night, unless you opt for the L20,000-per-night portable air-conditioning units, which most Cheap Sleepers won't want to do. When I visited the hotel, work was in progress to enlarge the breakfast room to accommodate 50 or more. This was done to appeal to the small groups that the hotel takes almost year round. For those living in the bathless rooms, the hall facilities are exceptionally nice and well maintained.

English Spoken: Yes

Facilities & Services: Air-conditioning (L20,000 per day), direct-dial phones, lift

Nearest Tourist Attractions: Campo de' Fiori, Piazza Navona

AREA
Campo de' Fiori

TELEPHONE
(06) 687.59.29

FAX
(06) 654.54.95 or 689.21.21

TELEX
None

NUMBER OF ROOMS
35; w/BST, 18; w/o BST, 17

CREDIT CARDS
AMEX, MC, V

RATES
Single L55,000–77,000; double L83,000–103,000; triple L100,000–130,000; quad L120,000–170,000; breakfast L5,000 extra

Hotel Teatro di Pompeo ★★★
Largo del Pallaro, 8

This hotel was built around the ruins of the Roman Theater of Pompey, where Julius Caesar was assassinated. Breakfast is served in the excavated cavelike remains of this ancient arena, and a sitting room is carved out of the cellars of the former theater. The Pompeo's 12 bright and spacious rooms rate high for charm, efficiency, and comfort, with their original wood-beamed ceilings and polished terracotta floors. The rustic decor, combined with blue cotton paisley bedspreads on firm mattresses, creates a very pleasing and welcoming air. The management is courteous, and the location near the Campo de' Fiori, the Pantheon, Piazza Navona, and good transportation to the train station and the Vatican is impossible to top.

AREA
Campo de' Fiori

TELEPHONE
(06) 687.25.66 or 687.28.12

FAX
(06) 654.55.31

TELEX
None

NUMBER OF ROOMS
12; all w/BST

CREDIT CARDS
AMEX, DC, MC, V

RATES
Single L198,000; double L231,000; triple L310,000; lower rates in Aug; breakfast included

English Spoken: Yes

Facilities & Services: Air-conditioning, bar, conference rooms, direct-dial phones, mini-bars, private room safes, TV

Nearest Tourist Attractions: Campo de' Fiori, Piazza Navona, Pantheon

COLISEUM

Hotel Colosseum ★★★
Via Sforza, 10

AREA
Coliseum

TELEPHONE
(06) 482.72.28, 482.73.12. or 474.34.86

FAX
(06) 482.72.85

TELEX
611151

NUMBER OF ROOMS
50; all w/BST

CREDIT CARDS
AMEX, DC, MC, V

RATES
Single L110,000; double L150,000; extra bed L35,000; group rates available on request; breakfast L15,000 extra per person

An impressive entryway with an arched wooden ceiling leads to a baronial sitting room, which is furnished in rustic reproductions that look as though they came from an old hunting lodge. There is a large breakfast room with well-spaced tables and leather chairs where you start your day, and a little bar upstairs where you can recover nicely from it. Heavy wooden furniture, wrought-iron wall lights, and plain wood or tile floors are found in all the rooms, which are missing amenities such as televisions, radios, and luggage space. Many of the twin bed chambers redefine *small*, but if you are traveling light and in search of a room with a view, No. 74 overlooking the Coliseum is a stunning choice.

English Spoken: Yes

Facilities & Services: Air-conditioning (portable, L10,000 extra per day), bar, direct-dial phones, hair dryers, lift, TV (L10,000 extra per day)

Nearest Tourist Attractions: Coliseum, Forum, Santa Maria Maggiore Church

PANTHEON

Albergo Abruzzi ★★
Piazza della Rotunda, 69

AREA
Pantheon

TELEPHONE
(06) 679.20.21

FAX
None

At Albergo Abruzzi, you enter off the street directly across from the Pantheon, walk up a flight of marble stairs, and check into large rooms that show only a few chips here and there. Yes, there are exposed pipes, funny little folding bidets, no private toilets or showers, no lounge, breakfast is not served, and there is no carpeting in any of the bedrooms. But—the bottom line is that the rooms are clean; nothing is mismatched, torn, or stained; and if you are lucky and get a front room, your view will be directly onto the Pantheon. If you are planning on a summer visit, reserve at least one month in advance and secure your reservation with an international money order.

English Spoken: Yes

Facilities & Services: None

Nearest Tourist Attractions: Pantheon, Piazza Navona

TELEX
None

NUMBER OF ROOMS
25; w/BST, none; w/o BST, all

CREDIT CARDS
None; cash only

RATES
Single L50,000–60,000; double L80,000–90,000; triple L120,000; quad L150,000; no charge for showers

Albergo Cesàri ★★★
Via di Pietra, 89

The Cesàri is situated on a quiet street in the historic heart of Rome. Billing itself as the second-oldest hotel in Rome, it has been in business since 1787 and has long been a favorite of famous literary, historical, and political guests including Stendhal, Guiseppe Garibaldi, and Raumer. Anna Palumbo and her family have owned and run the hotel since the turn of the century. While they have upgraded the bathrooms to a certain extent, the hotel still retains its original feel and charm, thanks to the collection of antique furnishings, oil paintings in gold leaf frames, and a scattering of Oriental rugs in the public areas. For long stays, I recommend room No. 44, a two-room suite with a sitting room overlooking a quiet side street. Cheap Sleepers will enjoy a coffee bar across the street that serves wonderful coffees and pastries for about one third the price of breakfast taken at the hotel.

English Spoken: Yes

Facilities & Services: Air-conditioning L20,000 extra per room per day, bar, direct-dial phones, mini-bars, TVs

Nearest Tourist Attractions: Pantheon, Via del Corso, Temple of Neptune

AREA
Pantheon

TELEPHONE
(06) 679.23.86, 684.06.32, or 679.60.83

FAX
679.08.82

TELEX
None

NUMBER OF ROOMS
50; w/BST, 40; w/o BST, 10

CREDIT CARDS
AMEX, DC, MC, V

RATES
Single L140,000; double L160,000; triple L185,000; no charge for showers; discounted rates in off seasons; breakfast L15,000 extra per person, served in rooms only

Albergo del Sole al Pantheon ★★★
Piazza della Rotunda, 63

For a Big Splurge next to the Pantheon, Albergo del Sole al Pantheon is a standout choice. The hotel

AREA
Pantheon

TELEPHONE
(06) 678.04.41
FAX
(06) 684.06.89
TELEX
622649 CISAT
NUMBER OF ROOMS
30; all w/BST
CREDIT CARDS
AMEX, DC, MC, V
RATES
Single L275,000; double
L400,000; triple and suites
L450,000; discounts on
weekends and in Aug; large
cold buffet breakfast and bacon
and eggs included

has been completely renovated, and no detail has been overlooked in providing every creature comfort. The stunning entry leads guests by a stone desk to an atrium garden along the back wall. There is an intimate bar for a quiet rendezvous, and a beautiful sitting room dominated by a large marble fireplace. All the rooms are beautifully appointed and equipped with everything from fluffy terry cloth towels and robes to private safes and well-stocked mini-bars. The furnishings are top-quality antiques and reproductions, the colors are coordinated, and space is abundant. Several baths boast Jacuzzis. My favorites are the Federico III, a large suite with a separate entry, a comfortable sofa, a built-in bar and television, and a lovely polished walnut desk; and the Caliostro, a double with a painted ceiling, a red stone floor, and two built-in wardrobes. A filling breakfast featuring your choice of cold cereals, yogurt, fresh fruit, and bacon and eggs cooked to your preference is included. If you do not want to go downstairs to eat in the morning, room service will be happy to bring your breakfast to you.

Note: The Piazza della Rotunda is one of the most beautiful and busiest squares in Rome. It is also one of the noisiest. If a room with a view is a must, bring earplugs. If calm is what you crave, ask for a room on the back where the view won't inspire, but the quiet will.

English Spoken: Yes

Facilities & Services: Air-conditioning (included), bar, direct-dial phones, hair dryers, lift, mini-bars, private room safes, room service, radios, TVs, some Jacuzzis, laundry service

Nearest Tourist Attractions: Pantheon, Piazza Navona, Via del Corso, Piazza Venezia

PIAZZA DEL POPOLO

Albergo Fiorella ★
Via del Babuino, 196

AREA
Piazza del Popolo

No keys after a 1 A.M. lockout, no lift, and no rugs on the floor, just noise and rock-bottom prices are what you can expect at the one-star Albergo Fiorella. To reach it, you must ring the bell on the street and climb up a drab marble staircase to the first-floor door where Signora Albano will let you in, as she has all her guests for the last 40 years. When I was there it was in late January and she was wearing a fur coat and boots. Money is not wasted on heating this eight-room spot only minutes away from Piazza del Popolo, the Spanish Steps, and wildly expensive boutique shopping. She is a friendly hostess who lives on the premises, does all the hard work herself, and is sweet and gentle—unless she catches you pulling some sort of hanky panky such as washing in your room or having nonpaying overnight visitors. Then the storm clouds gather and you will probably be asked to find other accommodations.

English Spoken: Very limited

Facilities & Services: None

Nearest Tourist Attractions: Piazza del Popolo, Spanish Steps, Via Condotti

Hotel Locarno ★★★
Via della Penna, 22

Since 1925, the family-owned Locarno, tucked between Piazza del Popolo and the Tiber, has been drawing a faithful clientele of international guests. The beautiful Belle Époque lobby and sitting room with a bar to one side display beveled glass doors, dark wood paneling, and an impressive collection of Tiffany lamps. A side garden with huge umbrellas is the perfect spot for summer breakfasts or cool afternoon drinks. Subway and bus stops and several good restaurants (see *Cheap Eats in Italy*) are within easy walking distance from the hotel door. The charming rooms, all of which face out, vary in size and are nicely appointed with antiques and floral-print draperies and spreads. Even the smallest single has enough space to unpack and stay a while. If there is a drawback to the hotel, it would be the dated bathrooms with their curtainless showers. Plans are now in the works to redo these, and hopefully when you arrive, the bathrooms will have been revamped.

TELEPHONE
(06) 361.05.97

FAX
None

TELEX
None

NUMBER OF ROOMS
8; w/BST, none; w/o BST, all

CREDIT CARDS
None

RATES
Single L45,000; double L75,000; breakfast included

011-39-6

AREA
Piazza del Popolo

TELEPHONE
(06) 361.08.41/2/3 or 361.08.60

FAX
(06) 321.52.49

TELEX
622251 HOTLOC I

NUMBER OF ROOMS
38; all w/BST

CREDIT CARDS
AMEX, MC, V

RATES
Single L155,000; double L225,000; triple L290,000; breakfast included

For the athletically inclined and *very* brave souls who are willing to venture into the crazy Roman traffic, the hotel provides free bicycles for guests to use during their stay.

English Spoken: Yes

Facilities & Services: Air-conditioning, bar, direct-dial phones, hair dryers, mini-bars, lift, parking (L30,000 per day), room service, TV, free bicycles

Nearest Tourist Attractions: Piazza del Popolo, Tiber

Hotel Margutta ★★
Via Laurina, 34

AREA
Piazza del Popolo

TELEPHONE
(06) 322.36.74

FAX
None

TELEX
None

NUMBER OF ROOMS
24; all w/BST

CREDIT CARDS
AMEX, DC, MC, V

RATES
1 or 2 persons L125,000; triple L150,000; breakfast included

Nothing is frilly, fancy, or fantastic at the Hotel Margutta. We are talking back-to-basics here in an old hotel on a quiet street in a good location near the Piazza del Popolo. I will admit that my first impression was not good. However, after inspecting the spotless rooms with their soundproofed windows and overcoming the questionable mix of fabric patterns and colors, my confidence was restored and I can recommend this as a modestly priced stopover for budgeteers. The three top-floor rooms have good views, and all rooms in the hotel have private bathrooms. No, they are not large, nor do they display the latest word in design technology, but you don't have to shuffle down the hall in search of the shower, or stand in line to wait your turn once you get there.

English Spoken: Yes

Facilities & Services: Lift

Nearest Tourist Attractions: Piazza del Popolo, Spanish Steps, shopping

Residenza Brotzky ★★
Via del Corso, 509 (to reach the Residenza from the street, take the lift in the courtyard to the third floor, where you will find the reception desk)

AREA
Piazza del Popolo

TELEPHONE
(06) 361.23.39, or 323.66.41

Young-at-heart romantics looking for a threadbare hotel experience in Rome will love the Residenza Brotzky. Housed in a 300-year-old building with stained-glass windows, winding staircases, and furniture from the twenties and thirties in need of some TLC, this popular spot is packed from April to September with young international travelers who are willing to trade comfort and style for camaraderie and funky charm. Large doses of tolerance and understanding are required to overlook the peeling and water-stained wallpaper, the chipped paint, the bare light bulbs, the low metal camp-style beds, and the sagging curtains that grace most of the 24 rooms. Some of the rooms, however, have had a recent coat of paint and have new mattresses. A few have private balconies, and most have showers. An outdoor staircase leads to a rooftop garden with a panoramic view of Rome. Many of the faithful return for this alone, and, I will admit, watching the sun set from this high perch above Rome while sipping a glass of wine with the one you love *is* an experience you will always remember.

English Spoken: Most of the time

Facilities & Services: Lift

Nearest Tourist Attractions: Piazza del Popolo, shopping, Via Condotti, Spanish Steps

PIAZZA NAVONA

Hotel Genio ★★★
Via Zanardelli, 28

From the moment I walked into this attractive hotel, I could see that it would soon be on my short list of favorite hotels in Rome. Well managed and beautifully maintained from top to bottom by Giuseppe di Gregorio, the hotel offers a friendly Italian atmosphere along with comfort and good value. The location is great, just north of Piazza Navona, one of Rome's loveliest squares. For trips farther afield, there is a taxi stand across the street and a bus stop at the corner with service to the train station and the Coliseum. The neutral bedrooms are carefully and neatly furnished, with Oriental rugs tossed on polished tile floors, creamy furniture with hand-done floral accents, and remodeled baths. Little bowls of candies and packets of stationery add

FAX
None

TELEX
None

NUMBER OF ROOMS
24; w/BST, 10; w/o BST, 14

CREDIT CARDS
None

RATES
Single L40,000–60,000; double L70,000–90,000; L25,000 each extra person; breakfast served only for groups

AREA
Piazza Navona

TELEPHONE
(06) 654.72.46 or 683.21.91

FAX
(06) 654.72.46

TELEX
623651

NUMBER OF ROOMS
61; all w/BST

CREDIT CARDS
AMEX, DC, MC, V

RATES
Single L165,000; double L245,000; extra bed L70,000; breakfast buffet included

welcoming and convenient touches. The rooftop solarium offers guests a fabulous bird's-eye view of Rome that encompasses the Villa Borghese, the Observatory, Castel St. Angelo, St. Peter's, Piazza Venezia, and the Pantheon.

English Spoken: Yes

Facilities & Services: Some air-conditioned rooms, direct-dial phones, hair dryers, lift, TVs

Nearest Tourist Attractions: Piazza Navona, Tiber, Pantheon

Hotel Piccolo ★★
Via dei Chiavari, 32

AREA
Piazza Navona

TELEPHONE
(06) 654.25.60 or 689.23.30

FAX
None

TELEX
None

NUMBER OF ROOMS
15; w/BST, 3; w/o BST, 12

CREDIT CARDS
None

RATES
Single L50,000; double L75,000–95,000; triple L100,000

Signor and Signora Riversi's Hotel Piccolo is a newly redone, quiet, spotlessly clean choice near Piazza Navona. The small rooms have bare floors, floral bedspreads, ultra-modern styleless furniture, and zip in the charm department. However, the prices are right, the welcome is warm, and the location off Corso Vittorio Emanuele is one of the best and most central in Rome. Breakfast is not served, but there are many *caffès* nearby where you can mix with the locals.

English Spoken: Very little

Facilities & Services: None

Nearest Tourist Attractions: Piazza Navona, Campo de' Fiori, Piazza Farnese

Hotel Portoghesi ★★★
Via dei Portoghesi, 1

AREA
North of Piazza Navona

TELEPHONE
(06) 686.42.31 or 654.51.33

FAX
(06) 687.69.76

TELEX
None

NUMBER OF ROOMS
27; all w/BST

CREDIT CARDS
MC, V

RATES
Single L100,000; double L140,000–170,000; suite L225,000; breakfast included

The hotel and street it is on take their name from the neighboring National Portuguese Church of St. Anthony. The central setting is marvelous, right in the heart of historic Old Rome near Piazza Navona and the Pantheon. A tiny lobby with a miniscule lift are the guest's first impressions of this 150-year-old hotel, where no two rooms are alike but all are comfortably broken in, just like your favorite pair of slippers. Most of them would benefit from some redecorating, either by coordinating the paint, blending the fabrics, or updating the bathrooms and adding some shelf space. Scattered antiques throughout, rooms with views, a rooftop terrace with wonderful vistas of ancient Rome, and quiet rooms along the back all help to make this a popular choice, despite its eclectic interior.

English Spoken: Yes

Facilities & Services: Air-conditioning, direct-dial phones, hair dryer in most rooms, lift, TVs

Nearest Tourist Attractions: Piazza Navona, Pantheon, Tiber

Pensione Navona ★
Via dei Sediari, 8

Despite a long list of posted rules, the management is accommodating at this one-star pensione housed in a 14th-century palazzo in central Rome. Some of the rules guests must follow: payment must be made in advance; you must leave your room each day by 10 A.M.; no visitors, candles, or laundry are permitted in the rooms; and maid service is not available on Sunday. You can see that Australian owner Corry Natale runs a tight ship. He is a graduate of Notre Dame and came to Rome over 20 years ago to study architecture and never left. Now he and his family own and operate this popular spot geared to student groups from Iowa, California, Florida, and Arizona. The rooms are rather boring and the towels can be threadbare, but for the price, you can't expect the Ritz. One benefit you will have if you stay here is the option of hiring their Mercedes to transport you to and from the airport for L60,000 a trip. Since most taxis cost at least L80,000 for the same ride, this is a deal well worth serious consideration, especially if there are several people in your party.

English Spoken: Yes

Facilities & Services: Lift to only 2 floors

Nearest Tourist Attractions: Piazza Navona, Piazza di S. Eustachio, Pantheon

AREA
Piazza Navona

TELEPHONE
(06) 686.42.03 or 654.38.02

FAX
None

TELEX
None

NUMBER OF ROOMS
30; w/BST, 27; w/o BST, 3

CREDIT CARDS
None

RATES
Single L70,000; double L95,000; triple L120,000, extra person in room, L38,000 per day; breakfast included (limited to 1 cup of coffee or tea and 1 roll)

PIAZZA VENEZIA

Coronet Hotel Pensione ★
Piazza Grazioli, 5

Big old-fashioned rooms with high wooden ceilings, exposed plumbing pipes, dust here and there,

AREA
Piazza Venezia

TELEPHONE
(06) 679.23.41

FAX
None

TELEX
None

NUMBER OF ROOMS
13; w/BST, 3; w/o BST, 10

CREDIT CARDS
AMEX, V

RATES
Single L80,000–90,000; double
L100,000–125,000; triple
L145,000–165,000; quad
L190,000–225,000; breakfast
included

bare floors, and nondescript furniture characterize this one-star Cheap Sleep on the third floor of the Palazzo Doria. In the bargain, expect some noise, not so much from the street as through the tissue-thin walls of your room. Hopefully you won't mind what your neighbor has on the radio, and you will be invited to join the room parties that seem to be taking place almost around the clock. As you can see, management is *very* tolerant. No, of course it is not the place for uptight types, but for a young-at-heart group of three or four traveling together, it is a good bet in a central location with prices that won't melt down a credit card.

English Spoken: Most of the time

Facilities & Services: Lift to hotel

Nearest Tourist Attractions: Piazza Venezia, Piazza Navona, Pantheon

Tiziano Hotel ★★★
Corso Vittorio Emanuele, 110

AREA
Piazza Venezia

TELEPHONE
(06) 686.50.19

FAX
(06) 686.50.19

TELEX
623697 TIZ HTL

NUMBER OF ROOMS
52; all w/BST

CREDIT CARDS
AMEX, DC, MC, V

RATES
Single L160,000; double
L210,000; triple L260,000;
discounts on weekends and
from Aug 1–Sept 15; buffet
breakfast included

The elegant 18th-century Pacelli Palace, still owned today by the family of Pope Pius XII, houses the aristocratic Hotel Tiziano. The location on the impossibly busy Corso Vittorio Emanuele will be noisy unless you keep the double-glazed windows shut, bring industrial-strength earplugs, or request a back room without a view. The hotel is professionally run and very well kept. It is also one of the few three-star hotels with a restaurant, good for those who are too exhausted to venture out on their own. All the rooms are the same, with off-white walls and pale green and beige bedspreads. Some have wooden floors, but those on the front have carpeting. There is a pleasant downstairs sitting area with marble floors, soft leather chesterfield couches, and a bar. A buffet breakfast is included in the room price, and, if you eat well, it should keep you going until dinner, with time out for a *gelato* in the afternoon.

English Spoken: Yes

Facilities & Services: Air-conditioning, bar, direct-dial phones, hair dryers, mini-bars, lift, parking

(L25,000 per day), restaurant for all meals, room service, TVs (must ask for remote control)

Nearest Tourist Attractions: Piazza Navona, Campo de' Fiori, Pantheon

SPANISH STEPS

Hotel Carriage ★★★
Via delle Carrozze, 36

The Carriage is one of my favorite hotels near the Spanish Steps. Classically furnished with lovely antiques throughout, the pale blue and gold decor creates a soothing and elegant feeling in this impeccable hotel. The rooms are on the small side, but beautifully coordinated, with attractive furniture and way-above-average bathrooms. Many of the bedrooms have their own terraces, with sweeping views over the rooftops of Rome and the Spanish Steps. Two top-floor rooms open directly onto a rooftop garden, where guests gather at the American Bar for al fresco breakfasts in the morning and sunset views in the evening. Long a favorite with French Embassy personnel and an occasional film star, rooms here are in high demand, making reservations essential as far in advance as possible.

English Spoken: Yes

Facilities & Services: Air-conditioning, bar, direct-dial phones, hair dryers, mini-bars, lift (does not service roof garden or rooms opening onto it), room service for snacks until 11 P.M., TVs, radios

Nearest Tourist Attractions: Spanish Steps

AREA
Spanish Steps
TELEPHONE
(06) 679.33.12 or 679.31.52
FAX
(06) 678.82.79
TELEX
626246 KINGHO I
NUMBER OF ROOMS
24; all w/BST
CREDIT CARDS
AMEX, DC, MC, V
RATES
Single L215,000;
double L275,000;
suite for 2 L300,000;
suite for 4 L350,000; seasonal discounts; breakfast included

Hotel Condotti ★★★
Via Mario de' Fiori, 37

The Condotti is a bright, serviceable address to remember if you want to be near the Spanish Steps, luxury shopping, and good restaurants in all price ranges (see *Cheap Eats in Italy* for suggestions).

Totally revamped at the end of 1991, the hotel is now a well-balanced mixture of the old and new. This is especially true in the lobby, where contemporary

AREA
Spanish Steps
TELEPHONE
(06) 679.46.61 or 679.47.96;
toll-free from U.S. 1-800-448-8355
FAX
(06) 679.04.84

TELEX
None

NUMBER OF ROOMS
17; all w/BST

CREDIT CARDS
AMEX, DC, MC, V

RATES
Single L160,000; double
L215,000; triple L280,000;
breakfast included

overstuffed sofas strewn with brightly colored pillows mix nicely with inlaid antique tables and chests. A large breakfast consisting of cereal, cheese, salami, yogurt, a basket of rolls, and hot beverages should get you off to the right start for a hard day of Roman sightseeing. The rooms are designer-coordinated, with pearl gray and blue carpeting, seafoam blue draperies, and laminated burled-wood furniture surfaces. The baths are adequate, with good lighting and fast-drying cotton towels. The basic singles are tiny, but even worse is to be stuck in a single that is being used as a double. These rooms are definitely to be avoided. Room No. 204, with a small entry, built-ins, and street view is a favorite. An added bonus is the hotel's toll-free Utell 800 number, which allows reservations to be made from any place in the United States.

English Spoken: Yes

Facilities & Services: Air-conditioning and sound proofing, bar, direct-dial phones, lift, TVs

Nearest Tourist Attractions: Spanish Steps, shopping on Via Condotti and in neighborhood

Hotel Doge ★★
Via due Macelli, 106

AREA
Spanish Steps

TELEPHONE
(06) 678.00.38

FAX
(06) 679.16.33

TELEX
None

NUMBER OF ROOMS
11; all w/BST

CREDIT CARDS
DC, MC, V

RATES
Single L85,000; double
L120,000; triple L162,000;
lower rates Oct–April; breakfast
included

The knockout location puts you in the heart of things around the Spanish Steps, the management is friendly, and for the area the prices are competitive. The reception area and lounge can best be described as *flossy*, with cut velvet fabric on the reproduction Victorian sofas and low chairs. To one side is a tiny espresso bar, and in the center of things is a television set running nonstop. The baths, added as an afterthought in some rooms, remind me of train-style cubicles, but they are clean and each has a fan. The rooms display a touch of orange here and there, but are tidy and without glaring gouges. Nothing matches, and I am talking different patterns on the bedspreads, curtains, chairs, tablecloths, and, in some cases, two types of wallpaper in the same room. Well, it is a two-star without upgrades and, who knows, by the time you arrive, something may have been done to alleviate the nightmare-inducing decorating scheme.

English Spoken: Yes

Facilities & Services: Direct-dial phones, lift

Nearest Tourist Attractions: Spanish Steps, Trevi Fountain, shopping, Via del Corso

Hotel Gregoriana ★★★
Via Gregoriana, 18

Very friendly and personalized service is the keynote at the Gregoriana, in a dynamite location only a whisper away from the famed Hotel Hassler and the top of the Spanish Steps. The Art Deco–style hotel is a popular destination for Valentino models and other high-fashion types. The 19th-century building was originally occupied by an order of nuns, and Room C still has some remnants of the original chapel. A black and gold birdcage elevator carries guests from the tiny lobby area to their floors, which are done in leopard- or English Liberty–print wallpaper or covered in bamboo. There are no public rooms; thus breakfast is served in your room or on your terrace, if you have one. The rooms are all identified with fanciful Erté letter prints on the doors and are decorated in a Chinese motif with red lacquer furniture set against stark white walls. Tiny balconies wrapped in wisteria vines offer pretty cityscape views. For the best of these, ask for Room R or S.

English Spoken: Yes

Facilities & Services: Air-conditioning, lift, parking (L30,000 per day), room service for bar beverages, TVs

Nearest Tourist Attractions: Spanish Steps, good shopping on Via Condotti

AREA
Spanish Steps

TELEPHONE
(06) 679.42.69

FAX
(06) 678.42.58

TELEX
None

NUMBER OF ROOMS
19; all w/BST

CREDIT CARDS
None

RATES
Single L156,000; double L220,000–230,000; triple L250,000; no discounts at any time; breakfast included

Hotel Internazionale ★★★
Via Sistina, 79

Occupying a prime patch of real estate near the Spanish Steps, the Internazionale is one of Rome's best moderately priced hotels. Your day will begin with breakfast served in a dining room with a high ceiling, lacy Venetian glass chandeliers, and an inlaid

AREA
Spanish Steps

TELEPHONE
(06) 678.46.86, 678.47.64, or 679.30.47

terra-cotta floor. The tables are covered with white linens, and seating is on comfortable, cushioned chairs. The dining room adjoins a massive sitting room with an impressive carved wood ceiling, groupings of leather chairs and couches, and a huge wood-burning fireplace. The third-floor public area resembles an old hunting lodge, with displays of armor, spears, and other antique hunting paraphernalia. The compact, pastel-toned rooms have double-glazed windows to buffer the Roman traffic noise, color television, mini-bars, air-conditioning (included in the price of the room), and private safes. The rooms on the fourth floor come with their own private terraces and lovely views over the nearby rooftops. The bathrooms are equipped with terry towels, assorted toiletries, and a radio. The management is crisply professional and to the point.

English Spoken: Yes

Facilities & Services: Air-conditioning included, direct-dial phones, hair dryers, mini-bars, lift, private room safes, room service (drinks) until 9 P.M., TVs with satellite, radios

Nearest Tourist Attractions: Spanish Steps, Via Condotti, Via Veneto, boutique shopping

Hotel King ★★★
Via Sistina, 131

For a good deal less than many of its neighbors charge, you will get a proper room and cordial service at the professionally managed King. Even though most of the rooms are large by Roman standards, they are done in the universal hotel style encountered from Detroit to Dubai. Most rooms have nice street views, and all have air-conditioning and color television. The baths are adequate, but you will have to contend with cotton towels that get wet fast and stay that way too long. The panoramic view from the roof garden is inspiring, and so is the hotel's location close to the Spanish Steps and many good restaurants (see *Cheap Eats in Italy*). Room service is available for breakfast and light snacks in the afternoon.

English Spoken: Yes

FAX
(06) 678.47.64
TELEX
614333 Inhot-1
NUMBER OF ROOMS
42; all w/BST
CREDIT CARDS
AMEX, MC, V
RATES
Single L175,000; double L250,000; triple L340,000; suite or apt L420,000–500,000; breakfast included in price of room

AREA
Spanish Steps
TELEPHONE
(06) 482.15.67 or 488.08.78
FAX
(06) 487.18.13
TELEX
626246 KINGHO I
NUMBER OF ROOMS
72; all w/BST
CREDIT CARDS
AMEX, DC, MC, V
RATES
Single L160,000–175,000; double L220,000; triple L255,000; suites L330,000; breakfast included

Facilities & Services: Air-conditioning, bar, direct-dial phones, some hair dryers, lift, parking (L25,000–37,000 depending on car size), room service for light snacks, TVs, some radios

Nearest Tourist Attractions: Spanish Steps, shopping

Hotel Manfredi ★★★
Via Margutta, 61

If your budget is flexible and you are looking for contemporary efficiency in a classy location close to fine shops and good restaurants, the Manfredi will suit you. A stylish renovation project four years ago turned this tired third-floor pensione into an attractive three-star hotel with every comfort and service one expects when paying top lire. The small downstairs reception area, bar, and eating area have pink marble floors accented with pink-striped furniture coverings and fresh flowers on the breakfast tables. The rooms upstairs are uniformly turned out in shades of gray and pink. The tiled baths have good lighting and enough space for more than just a razor and a toothbrush. The number of repeat customers is growing, and it is easy to see why. All the rooms are quiet, discounts are given in winter and summer seasons, and the management is always attentive and helpful.

English Spoken: Yes

Facilities & Services: Air-conditioning, direct-dial phones, hair dryers, mini-bars, lift, TVs, radio, laundry service available

Nearest Tourist Attractions: Piazza del Popolo, Spanish Steps, Via Condotti, art galleries, Tiber

AREA
Spanish Steps

TELEPHONE
(06) 320.76.76 or 320.76.95

FAX
(06) 320.77.36

TELEX
None

NUMBER OF ROOMS
17; all w/BST

CREDIT CARDS
AMEX, MC, V

RATES
Single L190,000; double L240,000; triple L300,000; good discounts Nov–Feb and July 15–Aug 31; American breakfast buffet with ham, cheese, eggs, etc., included

Hotel Pensione Erdarelli and Hotel Pensione Pierina ★★
Via Due Macelli, 28 and 47

You can arrange for dental care, seek legal advice, or plan a spur-of-the-moment trip to Africa at the dentist, lawyer, and Kenya Airways offices on the first floor of the building where the Erdarelli and its older sister the Pierina are located. The clean rooms vary

AREA
Spanish Steps

TELEPHONE
(06) 679.12.65 or 678.40.10

FAX
(06) 679.07.05

TELEX
None
NUMBER OF ROOMS
37; w/bst, 21; w/o bst, 16
CREDIT CARDS
AMEX, MC, V
RATES
Single L80,000–105,000;
double L125,000–145,000;
triple L165,000–200,000; 20%
discount Nov–Apr; breakfast
included

widely in both locations. Some have only a basin with hot and cold water taps; others have the works, including balconies. Those on the front will be impossibly noisy. The best single is No. 14 at the Erdarelli; it has its own bath and balcony. The top double, No. 32, featuring a sitting room and a marble floor but no private facilities, is also at the Erdarelli. Breakfast for both pensiones is served in the Erdarelli dining room, a large room with a signed photo of George Bush dedicated to the Erdarelli family, which has been at the helm of these two way stations for more than 50 years. No, George did not sleep here, but one of his staffers did. All in all, it is nothing to write home about, but at lower off-season rates, it does qualify as a Cheap Sleep in the heart of Rome.

English Spoken: Yes

Facilities & Services: Air-conditioning L20,000 extra per day, lift, laundry service

Nearest Tourist Attractions: Spanish Steps, shopping, Trevi Fountain

Hotel Pensione Parlamento ★★
Via delle Convertite, 5

AREA
Between Spanish Steps and
Trevi Fountain
TELEPHONE
(06) 679.20.82 or 678.78.80
FAX
None
TELEX
None
NUMBER OF ROOMS
22; w/bst, 14; w/o bst, 8
CREDIT CARDS
None
RATES
Single L60,000–80,000;
double L80,000–105,000;
L30,000 extra for each
additional person in room;
breakfast L14,000 extra

The first floor of this building owned by INA, the largest insurance company in Italy, is occupied by a tailor. The second floor houses Parliament offices, and on the third through the fifth floors is the Hotel Pensione Parlamento. To reach the hotel you must climb 77 steep steps that haven't been cleaned in years. There is a dispute going on between the tenants and landlord as to who is responsible for stair maintenance, and until it is solved, no one is willing to accept stair-cleaning duties. However, for those budget seekers in search of a Cheap Sleep in a good location, the hike is worth the effort because the hotel is nice and clean, and the owner really tries his level best to please all his guests. For the best results, ask for one of the 11 newly redone rooms on the fourth floor overlooking the flowering roof garden. In Room No. 108, a large double, you can see the belltower of the San Silvestro Church. If you land in No. 82, you will be in a large family room furnished with black marble-topped furniture and have your own shower and toilet. Breakfast is served on request, but for the price, you can certainly do better rubbing shoulders with the natives over a morning espresso or cappuccino at one of the bars in the neighborhood.

English Spoken: Yes

Facilities & Services: Private safe in all new rooms

Nearest Tourist Attractions: Spanish Steps, Via del Corso, shopping, Trevi Fountain

Hotel Pension Suisse ★★
Via Gregoriana, 54

The Hotel Pension Suisse is a typical Roman pensione on the fourth and fifth floors of an old building. There are no visible signs of upgrades, and little care has been devoted to developing any style or charm with the furnishings, which are mired in the fifties. The bare floors creak, the bidets are portable (!), and some showers are just a spout in the ceiling with no place for the water to go but all over everything in the bathroom. The pensione used to be bigger, but it lost its lease recently on over half of its space, so is now reduced to 13 rooms. As owner Yole Ciucci lamented to me, "Everything is so complicated; it is just part of the Italian mind set." So why should Cheap Sleepers stay here? For several reasons: it has an unbeatable location near the Spanish Steps, it is clean, no charges are levied for showers in the bathless roosts, and there is an elevator that works at least 80 percent of the time. Finally, if you are lucky and snare a top-floor room, you will have a view. The prices are low for the area, and they include a Continental breakfast with juice. In the off seasons, be sure to negotiate a discount.

English Spoken: Yes

Facilities & Services: Lift, some rooms with TV

Nearest Tourist Attractions: Spanish Steps, Trevi Fountain, shopping, Via Veneto

AREA
Spanish Steps

TELEPHONE
(06) 678.61.72

FAX
(06) 678.12.58

TELEX
None

NUMBER OF ROOMS
13; w/BST, 9; w/o BST, 4

CREDIT CARDS
None

RATES
Single L65,000–85,000; double L98,000–130,000; triple L170,000; breakfast included

Hotel Scalinata di Spagna ★★★
Piazza Trinità dei Monti, 17

AREA
Spanish Steps

TELEPHONE
(06) 679.30.06 or 684.08.96

FAX
(06) 684.05.98

TELEX
None

NUMBER OF ROOMS
15; all w/BST

CREDIT CARDS
MC, V

RATES
Single L200,000; double
L260,000; triple L320,000;
discounts Jan & Feb; breakfast
included

The Scalinata di Spagna used to be on everyone's list of small, charming, inexpensive hotels in Rome. Since its transformation from a modest pensione to a three-star hotel, the prices have skyrocketed and it is no longer inexpensive. It is included here for those with bigger budgets who are seeking an efficiently run hotel with personalized service. The only thing that seems to have changed about the hotel is the prices. It still has a spectacular view from the flower-filled roof garden, where breakfast is served most of the year. The top-drawer location, directly across the street from the Hassler Hotel, where rates *start* at L500,000 per night, is within easy access to big-name shopping, good restaurants, and strolling or jogging in the Villa Borghese Gardens. Cacao, the resident parrot, remains on his perch by the reception desk where he loudly welcomes all the guests. The rooms are on the small side and no two are alike, but all are nicely accented with antiques. Number 15, opening onto the terrace, is a good selection and so is No. 11, with its peekaboo look at the Spanish Steps. Even though prices are no longer low, demand far exceeds supply because the hotel has developed the type of following where guests begin to plot their return visit long before checking out.

English Spoken: Yes

Facilities & Services: Air-conditioning, direct-dial phones, hair dryers, mini-bars, radios, clocks

Nearest Tourist Attractions: Spanish Steps, shopping, Villa Borghese Gardens

TRAIN STATION

Albergo Igea ★★
Via Principe Amedeo, 97

AREA
Train Station

TELEPHONE
(06) 446.69.13 or 446.69.11

FAX
(06) 446.69.11

The Albergo Igea is a terrific two-star hotel value without the usual two-star dimestore taste that is so prevalent in Rome. True, there are a few Naugahyde-covered sofas in the sitting room, but the hotel is generally nice and neat. The rooms have pretty wall coverings, tiled floors, coordinated bedspreads and curtains, desks and chairs, luggage racks, and adequate moving-around space. A few of the rooms are noisy, but none of the furnishings have glaring spots or big tears. The baths are large, but the shower has no curtain, which seems to be standard for one- and two-star bathrooms in Rome. The hotel is within walking distance of the train station and opera, and close to several good restaurants listed in *Cheap Eats in Italy.*

English Spoken: Yes

Facilities & Services: Direct-dial phones, lift

Nearest Tourist Attractions: Opera

TELEX
None

NUMBER OF ROOMS
42; all w/BST

CREDIT CARDS
MC, V

RATES
Single L85,000; double L115,000; triple L155,000; breakfast L9,000 per person

Hotel Adler ★★
Via Modena, 5

The sign by the mirror where you enter the second-floor Adler says: "Peace starts with a smile." You will find both peace and many smiles at this friendly mamma and papà hotel run by Sr. and Sra. Brando. The rooms are clean, cozy, and rather Spartan, but the sparcity of furniture is outweighed by the slightly larger rooms and reasonable prices. The colors match, and the bathrooms have shelf space—some even have shower curtains, a rare find in most hotels in Rome. From this address you are close to the Piazza Repubblica, Via Nazionale, the opera, and the train station, as well as a subway stop and good city bus connections. When you add up all the plus points at the Adler, it turns out to be a good value.

English Spoken: Yes

Facilities & Services: Lift

Nearest Tourist Attractions: Opera

AREA
Train Station

TELEPHONE
(06) 488.09.40

FAX
(06) 488.09.40

TELEX
None

NUMBER OF ROOMS
16; w/BST, 10; w/o BST, 6

CREDIT CARDS
MC, V

RATES
Single L83,000; double L96,000–124,000; triple L132,000–165,000; breakfast included

Hotel Britannia ★★★
Via Napoli, 64

The warmth of the welcome by reception manager Nicette Assa, the careful attention to details, and the personalized service by the staff add up to a winning combination at the Britannia. The hotel, located right off busy Via Nazionale and within walking distance of the train station, has been completely redone in an

AREA
Train Station

TELEPHONE
(06) 488.31.53 or 488.57.85

FAX
(06) 488.23.83

TELEX
611292
NUMBER OF ROOMS
32; all w/BST
CREDIT CARDS
AMEX, DC, MC, V
RATES
Single L200,000; double
L240,000; triple L300,000;
25% discounts on weekends,
during winter, and, if not full,
all summer; children up to 10
sharing parents' room free;
breakfast included

attractive modern style. Mirrored walls give the downstairs public areas an open and spacious feeling, while soft built-in sofas, masses of pillows, and a small bar create a sense of overall comfort. Upstairs the bedrooms are uniformly outfitted in beige, soft rose, and light blue color schemes. Four of the rooms have private, plant-filled balconies. The superb baths have digital clocks and radios, scales, plenty of toiletries and towels, hair dryers, and sunlamps. The singles tend to run small, but each has a double bed, all amenities, and a wonderful bathroom. Some rooms have airless interior views, so if you are at all claustrophobic, it is best to avoid these. The breakfast, which is included in the room price, is way above average in both quality and quantity. In addition to the usual coffee, tea, or hot chocolate and roll, it includes a choice of three or four cakes, cheese, and fresh fruit juice.

English Spoken: Yes

Facilities & Services: Air-conditioning, bar, direct-dial phones, hair dryers, mini-bars, lift, private room safes, TVs, radios, clocks, phones in bathrooms, sunlamps

Nearest Tourist Attractions: Opera, Via Veneto, Coliseum (30-minute walk)

Hotel Canada ★★★
Via Vicenza, 58

AREA
Train Station
TELEPHONE
(06) 445.77.70/1/2; toll-free
from U.S. (Utell International)
1-800-448-8355
FAX
(06) 445.07.49
TELEX
613037 CANADA I
NUMBER OF ROOMS
70; all w/BST
CREDIT CARDS
AMEX, DC, MC, V

The Hotel Canada, owned for years by the Pucci family, is affiliated with Utell International Hotels, and that fact alone tells you that certain standards must be met and kept. If the hotel were in a tonier neighborhood, it probably would cost half again as much and be twice as popular.

The downstairs areas are exceptional, from the piano lounge and bar with inviting sofas and overstuffed chairs, to the well-outfitted meeting rooms and a large dining room with tables big enough for buffet-breakfast place settings and a morning paper. The hotel is divided into older and renovated sections. You definitely want the newer rooms with their pretty, coordinated decor and attractive furniture. Number 101, a twin-bedded room, is one of the best, and so is No. 108, a junior suite with a separate sitting room off the bedroom. If you make your own reservations directly with the hotel (not through the 800 number), the management will pass the commission normally given to travel agents to you as a 10 percent savings. Be sure to ask for this.

English Spoken: Yes

Facilities & Services: Air-conditioning, bar, direct-dial phones, hair dryers, lift, laundry service, private room safes, room service for breakfast and bar drinks, radios, TVs, telephone in bath in newer rooms, 2 rooms for handicapped

Nearest Tourist Attractions: None; must use public transportation, but excellent bus service nearby

Hotel Elide ★★
Via Firenze, 50

Giovanni Roma, his wife, and their pretty daughter Rosalba run this excellent budget pensione, where 14 rooms on three floors are well cared for and neat as a pin. Room Nos. 16 and 18 have two of the most beautifully hand-painted ceilings you will encounter in any hotel at any price in Rome. Other rooms are definitely in the plain Jane category, with white wallpaper and dull furniture, but they are so clean you could eat off the floors. Numbers 25 and 26 connect with a private bathroom and are ideal for Cheap Sleeping families. Those rooms with private baths have good towels (not those thin cotton numbers), but don't look for any shower curtains because there aren't any. A nice Continental breakfast is served in a combination television-and-dining room with an ornate ceiling. It is a shame that the black laminated cafe tables and cane chairs aren't more in keeping with the opulent ceiling. The Romas take tremendous pride in their little pensione and do something each year to improve it. For a safe budget bet near the train station, it is on my short list of favorites.

RATES
Single L100,000; double L180,000; triple L230,000; suite L200,000; large buffet breakfast with meat, cereal, cheese, yogurt, juice, and one hot dish plus rolls and coffee

AREA
Train Station

TELEPHONE
(06) 474.13.67 or 488.39.77

FAX
None

TELEX
None

NUMBER OF ROOMS
14; w/BST, 9; w/o BST, 5

CREDIT CARDS
MC, V

RATES
Single L65,000–75,000; double L75,000–95,000; extra bed, add 35%; breakfast L5,000 extra

English Spoken: Yes; daughter speaks English

Facilities & Services: Direct-dial phones, lift in hotel, which is one floor above street

Nearest Tourist Attractions: Opera, Trevi Fountain

Hotel Fiorini ★★
Via Principe Amedeo, 62

AREA
Train Station

TELEPHONE
(06) 488.50.65

FAX
(06) 488.21.70

TELEX
None

NUMBER OF ROOMS
16; w/BST, 12; w/o BST, 4

CREDIT CARDS
AMEX, DC, MC, V

RATES
Single L90,000–110,000; double L100,000–160,000; extra person 35% more; lower off-season rates; large Continental breakfast included

Renato and Anna Carollo have a two-star winner on their hands with their newly remodeled fifth-floor Hotel Fiorini. The sprightly surroundings include well-planned bedrooms with modern furniture, nice bedspreads, and no frightening colors. The showers have curtains, but the towels could be better. A delicious breakfast with cereal, orange juice, and fresh fruit in addition to the usual rolls and coffee is served in the amicably small breakfast room. From this hotel you can walk over to the train station and jump on one of the many buses that are waiting to take you anywhere you want to go in Rome. The neighborhood also has several budget restaurants serving everything from pizza to *gelato* to fresh fish and pasta fixed ten ways (see *Cheap Eats in Italy*).

English Spoken: Yes

Facilities & Services: Air-conditioning in some rooms, direct-dial phones, lift, TVs

Nearest Tourist Attractions: Train station, where you can get a bus to any destination in Rome

Hotel Flavia ★★
Via Flavia, 42

AREA
Train Station

TELEPHONE
(06) 488.30.37 or 487.11.53

FAX
(06) 481.91.29

TELEX
None

NUMBER OF ROOMS
30; all w/BST

CREDIT CARDS
None

While the rooms have many comforts, there is no lift for this second-story hotel midway between the train station and the Via Veneto. Despite this inconvenience, the two-star restyled Flavia is a sound bet, with clean, uniform rooms at attractive prices, especially in the low seasons. The modern rooms are done in orange with gaily striped cotton bedspreads, uncarpeted floors, luggage racks, and nicer bathrooms than many three-star hotels can claim. The management is friendly, and someone who speaks English is always at the desk. While not *centralissimo*, the hotel is within walking distance of the Via Veneto, the Villa Borghese Gardens, the Spanish Steps, and all the A-rated shopping Rome has to offer.

English Spoken: Yes

Facilities & Services: Direct-dial phones, mini-bars, TVs

Nearest Tourist Attractions: Via Veneto, Spanish Steps, shopping

RATES
Single L90,000; double L125,000; triple L170,000; discounts in off seasons; breakfast included

Hotel Imperia ★★
Via Principe Amedeo, 9

At the family-owned Imperia, the rooms are cheerful, the colors bright and not clashing, there are no grim, brown, overstuffed, lumpy chairs lurking around, and the bathrooms are good for a two-star near the train station. Each bedroom has a nicely tiled floor, a picture, and a bowl of artificial flowers—well, they *are* trying. There is a lift, and some of the bathrooms have a hair dryer. A basic breakfast is served for 5,000 lire, but I recommend the more Italian experience of standing at the bar at a corner *caffè*, where you can polish your language skills or just listen and be happy you are in Rome this morning.

English Spoken: Enough

Facilities & Services: Direct-dial phones, lift, some hair dryers

Nearest Tourist Attractions: Coliseum and Forum, but they are quite a walk

AREA
Train Station

TELEPHONE
(06) 481.44.74

FAX
None

TELEX
None

NUMBER OF ROOMS
7; w/BST, 3; w/o BST, 4

CREDIT CARDS
None

RATES
Single L55,000–75,000; double L75,000–90,000; triple L95,000 (no private bathroom); breakfast L5,000 extra

Hotel Marcella ★★★
Via Flavia, 106

Finding a good hotel near a railway station in any major European city is never an easy task. Now, the search is narrowed in Rome, thanks to the handsomely remodeled Marcella. The transformation was so impressive that the hotel won the top award in its class from the Rome Tourist Board.

A garden setting has been created in the lobby with the use of mirrors, latticed walls, and green and white slipcovered furniture. Morning papers are given out with the buffet breakfast, which is served at tables set along a wall of white banquettes. In the summer,

AREA
Train Station

TELEPHONE
(06) 474.64.51; toll-free from U.S. 1-800-448-8355

FAX
(06) 481.58.32

TELEX
621351

NUMBER OF ROOMS
68; all w/BST

CREDIT CARDS
AMEX, DC, MC, V

RATES
Single L155,000; double
L225,000; triple L285,000;
discounted rates Nov 16–Mar
15; buffet breakfast included

you can eat under the shade of an umbrella on the roof garden with its commanding view over Rome. The contemporary rooms are well coordinated, with white laminated and chrome furniture. I like No. 314, with its soft-gray suedecloth-covered walls, indirect lighting, a large desk, and a nice bathroom with stacks of absorbent towels. Number 10 is a quiet single with a street view, pink suedecloth on the walls, and a floral carpet. The neighborhood is interesting for its market shops, which sell everything from meats and vegetables to bread and household items. Good restaurants are within easy reach (see *Cheap Eats in Italy*). Last but not least, reservations may be made in the comfort of your own home by dialing the toll-free number.

English Spoken: Yes

Facilities & Services: Air-conditioning, bar, direct-dial phones, hair dryers, mini-bars, lift, parking (L25,000–38,000 per day), room service, TVs, radios

Nearest Tourist Attractions: Borghese Gardens, Via Veneto

Hotel Patria ★★★
Via Torino, 37–37

AREA
Train Station

TELEPHONE
(06) 488.07.56, 481.82.54, or
487.18.03; toll free from U.S.
1-800-448-8355

FAX
(06) 481.48.72

TELEX
621582 Patria I

NUMBER OF ROOMS
50; all w/BST

CREDIT CARDS
AMEX, DC, MC, V

RATES
Single L135,000; double
L200,000; triple L275,000;
breakfast included

For the traveler who does not demand luxury but appreciates basic creature comforts, the renovated Patria offers 50 rooms to Rome voyagers who want to be situated near the train station.

The reception area is done in black glazed rattan, with turquoise walls and carpeting. The uniformly decorated rooms have easy-care laminated furniture, good-sized wardrobes with built-in drawers, and coordinated fabrics on the beds, chairs, and curtains. There is a desk in most rooms, but in many the television set is mounted at ceiling level, making viewing difficult unless you are lying flat on the bed. The bathrooms are decent, with showers and tub curtains, but watch out for those cotton dish towels masquerading as bath towels. Breakfast is served in a minute basement room with only six tables. If you want to eat your morning meal at the hotel, consider having it brought to your room.

English Spoken: Yes
Facilities & Services: Air-conditioning, direct-dial phones, hair dryers, lift, radios, TVs
Nearest Tourist Attractions: Via Veneto

Hotel Romae ★★
Via Palestor, 49

Francesco and Lucy Boccaforno have owned the Hotel Romae for eight years. Currently, Francesco is the vice-president of the Family Hotel and Restaurant Association in Italy. This group of independent hotel and restaurant owners joined forces to offer the best service, quality, and value possible to the public. In my research, I looked at almost every hotel in the group in Florence, Rome, and Venice, and all were far above average. The Hotel Romae is no exception.

The young and attractive Boccafornos take great pride in their hotel, and it shows everywhere you look. They are on board every day to see that everything runs as it should. In addition, they will book tours for you, obtain tickets to shows, and make sightseeing suggestions. Their English is perfect, and they make everyone feel at home.

The simple bedrooms with tiled floors, paisley-printed bedspreads, lacy white window curtains, and peach-colored walls pass every cleanliness test. Some of the rooms on the third floor are new and the best. These have ceiling fans and the newest bathrooms. A modern desk area with a little bar, and a combination sitting and breakfast room compose the public areas of the hotel. In the afternoons you may find the Boccafornos' children quietly doing their homework here or eating an after-school snack.

English Spoken: Yes
Facilities & Services: Air-conditioning (L20,000 extra per day), bar, direct-dial phones, hair dryers, TVs
Nearest Tourist Attractions: Not much; train station nearby, with buses to take you to every tourist destination in Rome

AREA
Train Station
TELEPHONE
(06) 446.35.54/5
FAX
(06) 445.20.24
TELEX
None
NUMBER OF ROOMS
22; all w/BST
CREDIT CARDS
AMEX, MC, V
RATES
Single L85,000; double L125,000; extra person pays 35% more; 20% discount for readers of *Cheap Sleeps in Italy*; breakfast included

Hotel Select ★★★
Via V. Bachelet, 6

AREA
Train Station

TELEPHONE
(06) 445.63.83 or 49.11.37

FAX
(06) 444.10.86

TELEX
None

NUMBER OF ROOMS
19; all w/BST

CREDIT CARDS
AMEX, MC, V

RATES
Off Season:
Single L115,000; double
L130,000; triple L165,000; apt
for 4 L195,000.
*High Season (Mar–June and
Sept–Oct):*
Single L185,000; double
L340,000; triple L395,000;
apt for 4 L325,000. Breakfast
buffet included (cereal, yogurt,
cheese, ham, hard-cooked eggs,
rolls, and tea or coffee)

Walter and Gregorio Pecoraro have taken an old has-been hotel and turned it into a shining three-star choice for travelers wanting to stay near the railway station. In the vigorous renovation project, great effort was made to give the hotel special interest and warmth. To do this, they kept the beautiful staircase with its wooden banister and wrought-iron grillwork, and the skylight over it. Double-glazed windows now ensure peace and quiet in the soft pastel-colored rooms, all of which are decorated with flair. Each has plenty of luggage space and adequate closets. The baths have tiled showers with curtains, or large tubs. Guests can eat breakfast or just relax in the center patio filled with fragrant jasmine bushes, bright geraniums, blooming roses, and a huge banana tree. The brothers go all out to please their guests and are building an impressive list of return customers. I was impressed with this hotel, and I think you will be too.

English Spoken: Yes

Facilities & Services: Air-conditioning, bar, direct-dial phones, hair dryers, TVs

Nearest Tourist Attractions: Train station, with buses to take you anyplace you want to go

Hotel Venezia ★★★
Via Varese, 18

AREA
Train Station

TELEPHONE
(06) 445.71.01 or 493.687

FAX
(06) 495.76.87

TELEX
None

NUMBER OF ROOMS
61; all w/BST

CREDIT CARDS
AMEX, DC, MC, V

Frankly, I cannot say enough about the Hotel Venezia, a top-notch selection in a business and residential neighborhood a few minutes from the train station. Owner Rosmarie Diletti and her daughter Patricia truly care about each of their guests and take a personal interest in their well-being. The hotel is personalized throughout with a museum-worthy collection of 15th-, 16th- and 17th-century antiques, all labeled to show their age, origin, and original usage. Everywhere you look there is something interesting that will catch your eye. When checking in, notice the picture of the bride and groom hanging over the desk. This is a painting of Signora

Diletti's mother- and father-in-law, done at the turn of the century. The breakfast buffet is laid out on a 15th-century altar and served on authentic Italian farmer tables. Some of the doors leading from the lounge area are from the 16th century, and the glass-topped table base in the sitting room was used to carry saints into villages during the same era. The rooms are done in reproduction furnishings befitting the style and feel of the rest of the hotel. Each has a Murano chandelier, heavy white curtains, and interesting framed prints hanging on the walls. The best rooms are on the higher floors, where the rooms are flooded with light and many have balconies providing perfect observation stations for watching the neighborhood life below. Special rates are available if you say when reserving that you are a *Cheap Sleep in Italy* reader, and show the book when checking in.

English Spoken: Yes

Facilities & Services: Air-conditioning (L25,000 extra), bar, direct-dial phones, hair dryers, mini-bars, lift, laundry service, radios, TVs

Nearest Tourist Attractions: Train station, with buses to all major tourist destinations

RATES
Single L130,000; double L180,000; triple L265,000; L10,000 discount if you mention *Cheap Sleeps in Italy* when reserving and show it when checking in; buffet breakfast included

TRASTEVERE

Pensione Esty ★
Viale Trastevere, 108

You will find some of the lowest prices in Rome at this unpretentious yet functional and very safe pensione slightly removed from the boisterous heart of Trastevere. You will be, however, still within walking distance of all the restaurants and nonstop nighttime activities Trastevere is famous for. While the rooms lack character, coordinated colors, and private facilities other than a basin and running water, they are clean and the mattresses are lump-free. Depending on who is at the desk, service can vary from cool and distant to helpful and friendly. Never mind—just take another look at those breathtakingly low prices and remember that this Cheap Sleep is tough to top.

AREA
Trastevere

TELEPHONE
(06) 588.12.02

FAX
None

TELEX
None

NUMBER OF ROOMS
10; w/BST, none; w/o BST, all

CREDIT CARDS
None

RATES
Single L40,000; double L58,000; triple L70,000

English Spoken: No
Facilities & Services: Lift to third-floor door of hotel
Nearest Tourist Attractions: Trastevere, Tiber

Pensione Manara ★
Via Luciano Manara, 25

AREA
Trastevere

TELEPHONE
(06) 581.47.13

FAX
None

TELEX
None

NUMBER OF ROOMS
5; w/BST, none; w/o BST, all

CREDIT CARDS
None

RATES
1 or 2 persons L58,000; double L58,000; triple L80,000; showers 3,000 each

"An oasis of peace in the heart of Trastevere" is the motto of Pensione Manara. If you know Trastevere, you know that peace and quiet are not two of its virtues, but I must say, this spot is about as good as you will get if you want both a Trastevere site *and* quiet. The five-room family-owned and -run pensione is a homey choice with considerable atmosphere and low rates for the level of comfort offered. The furnishings are simple, the wallpaper won't give you nightmares, and neither will the mattresses. No English is spoken, so this spot presents a perfect opportunity to brush up on your Italian. Best of all, the location puts you in the thick of things in the pulsating area, which is famous for its nighttime hedonism.

English Spoken: No
Facilities & Services: None
Nearest Tourist Attractions: Heart of Trastevere

VATICAN

Giuggioli Hotel ★
Via Germanico, 198

AREA
Vatican

TELEPHONE
(06) 324.21.13

FAX
None

TELEX
None

NUMBER OF ROOMS
5; w/BST, 1; w/o BST, 4

CREDIT CARDS
None

RATES
1 or 2 persons L65,000–80,000

One of Rome's crown jewels of clean, safe, and inexpensive hotels is the second-floor Giuggioli. There are only five rooms, overseen by a sweet Italian grandmother and her cat. As I approached the front door, which is up two flights of steps, I had my doubts. But once I saw the big rooms, each with at least one or two pieces of interesting furniture, and decided to ignore the wildly printed bed sheets, I was impressed. The most expensive double is the matrimonial suite, with fabulous marble-topped mahogany dressers and an enormous mirrored armoire. This is the only room with a private bath.

There are no public areas, but if you ask, you will probably be able to use the sitting room, which is crowded with mementos and bric-a-brac gathered over decades of living at the same address.

English Spoken: None
Facilities & Services: None
Nearest Tourist Attractions: Vatican and Vatican museums

Hotel Alimandi ★★
Via Tunisi, 8

There is no Sunday maid service, and the reception area is nothing to speak of, but despite these two minus points, the Alimandi is head and shoulders above most other two-star hotels in the vicinity. Paolo Alimandi owns not only the hotel but the entire building, which is unusual in Rome. To make sure that all runs smoothly, he is on the job every day, checking up on the maids, answering guests' questions, and providing helpful advice. On the fourth floor he has created an inviting garden, and on the roof there is a terrace with a nice view. The lounge has a large color television, a piano, and a bar for soft drinks. Rooms come with a built-in wardrobe, a desk and chair, and a tile floor. Unfortunately there are no bedspreads, only blankets covering the beds. The showers have curtains, a simple feature missing in all too many Italian hotels. For groups, special rates, meals, transfers, and tours can be arranged.

English Spoken: Yes
Facilities & Services: Direct-dial phones, hair dryers, TV and radio in rooms with private bath
Nearest Tourist Attractions: Vatican and Vatican museums

AREA
Vatican
TELEPHONE
(06) 384.548 or 318.404
FAX
(06) 314.457
TELEX
616219
NUMBER OF ROOMS
30; w/BST, 20; w/o BST, 10
CREDIT CARDS
AMEX, DC, MC, V
RATES
Single L58,000–75,000; double L75,000–95,000; triple L98,000–125,000; children under 12 free; breakfast L8,000 extra

Hotel Amalia ★★
Via Germanico, 66 (Angle Via OttaViano)

A well-priced find near the Vatican is the family-owned Hotel Amalia. Located on the second floor, it has 24 bedrooms suitable for the non-fussy traveler on a budget. The rooms are gradually being redone in Motel Moderne, with red chenille and cotton

AREA
Vatican
TELEPHONE
(06) 314.519, 372.19.68, or 316.407

FAX
(06) 380.168

TELEX
None

NUMBER OF ROOMS
24; w/BST, 8; w/o BST, 16

CREDIT CARDS
MC, V

RATES
Single L50,000–70,000;
double L80,000–110,000;
triple L100,000 (no shower or
toilet in room); no charge for
showers; breakfast L10,000
per person

bedspreads, tiled floors, fringed lampshades, and hard chairs. There are no tables or places to put things, other than the bedside tables and window ledges. The back views are depressing and grim, so it is important to insist on facing front. There will be some noise, but it isn't an all-night affair. Avoid at all costs Room No. 317, a dark double with a small window that faces a dreary blank wall. Breakfast is an extra 10,000 lire. My advice is to eat at a neighborhood bar for about one third of this hotel charge.

English Spoken: Yes

Facilities & Services: Direct-dial phones

Nearest Tourist Attractions: Vatican, Vatican museums

Hotel Columbus ★★★
Via della Conciliazione, 33

AREA
Vatican

TELEPHONE
(06) 686.48.74, 686.52.45,
686.54.35, 678.16.40, or
686.77.96

FAX
(06) 686.48.74, 686.52.45

TELEX
620096

NUMBER OF ROOMS
125; all w/BST

CREDIT CARDS
AMEX, DC, MC, V

RATES
Single L170,000–205,000;
double L220,000–270,000;
extra person in room L35,000–
55,000; half- and full-board
available; breakfast included,
for L50,000 per person! Ask to
have it deducted;
better yet, *insist!*

The Hotel Columbus is a mere stone's throw away from St. Peter's. The 125-room hotel, which was built as a palace 12 years before Columbus sailed for America, has ornate carved and frescoed ceilings, pillars and arches everywhere you look, massive antiques, and a serene garden courtyard where cool drinks are served in warm weather. Some of the rooms look directly onto the basilica; others face the busy Via Conciliazione, which leads directly to the Vatican. All rooms are good-sized, with ample closet and living space, and are furnished in keeping with the style and spirit of the building. The hotel, which at first glance looks much more expensive than it actually is, is a popular target for ecclesiastical tour-group pilgrims. The dining room is not recommended for lunch or dinner. See *Cheap Eats in Italy* for wiser choices in the area.

English Spoken: Yes

Facilities & Services: Air-conditioning, bar, direct-dial phones, hair dryers, mini-bars, lift, free parking, TV with CNN hookup, restaurant for all meals

Nearest Tourist Attractions: Vatican and Vatican museums

Hotel Sant'Anna ★★★
Borgo Pico, 134

The Hotel Sant'Anna scores high for charm, comfort, and its location only a few blocks from St. Peter's. The frescoed lobby with a small sitting room leading to a garden is reassuringly pristine, with the front door closely monitored by the reception desk. A large buffet breakfast that includes eggs and cheese is served in the basement dining room. An outdoor setting is achieved in the arched room by using yellow and green flowered tablecloths and trompe l'oeil paintings of Roman ruins on the walls. There is no lift to any of the four floors, but the climb is worth it, especially for the top-floor rooms with their own terraces. Bathrooms in all the rooms pamper you with marble showers, terry towels, good lighting, and up-to-date plumbing; some have heated towel racks. One of my favorite rooms is No. 25, a tastefully decorated room for two done in shades of blue with blue floral wallpaper. There are double wardrobes in the entry, two sofa beds, and a terrace with a rooftop view. Another top pick is No. 10, a cozy double with a glass-topped writing area, a mirrored wall with frosted lights mounted onto it, and a nice corner view of the garden below.

English Spoken: Yes

Facilities & Services: Air-conditioning, direct-dial phones, hair dryers, mini-bars, parking (L30,000 per day), radios, TVs; no lift

Nearest Tourist Attractions: Vatican

AREA
Vatican

TELEPHONE
(06) 654.18.82 or 654.16.02

FAX
(06) 654.87.17

TELEX
None

NUMBER OF ROOMS
20; all w/BST

CREDIT CARDS
AMEX, DC, MC, V

RATES
Single L135,000–175,000; double L165,000–225,000; triple L175,000–240,000; lower rates in Aug, Jan, and Feb; buffet breakfast included

Olympic Hotel ★★★
Via Properzio, 2A

The Olympic Hotel gets my vote as one of the best hotels near the Vatican. It has been magnificently redone with style and verve while keeping the comfort of the guest its number-one priority.

The bedrooms have a personalized decorator look, with crisp linen bed coverings, built-in glass-topped desks, and fabric-covered walls. Number 302, with its soft charcoal-gray walls, is an exceptionally good choice. A corner room with two double-glazed

AREA
Vatican

TELEPHONE
(06) 689.66.50/2/3

FAX
(06) 654.82.55

TELEX
623368 OLYHTL I

NUMBER OF ROOMS
54; all w/BST

CREDIT CARDS
AMEX, DC, MC, V
RATES
Single L150,000; double
L232,000; triple L250,000;
suite L400,000; discounts in
Jan, Feb; breakfast included

windows, it has a curved burled-wood desk, matching curtains and bedspreads, and pretty ginger jar bedside lamps. The modern bathroom has marble and tile, with Lucite towel racks and a rolling cart for toiletry storage. The refined downstairs lobby and sitting rooms have large gilt mirrors, a massive marble table, and two large paintings, creating an elegant and appealing setting. Adding to the look are beige-striped sofas and black leather Directoire chairs. The hotel is professionally managed by a team of multilingual personnel. An interesting non-tourist-infested market operates daily on Via Cola Rienzo, just a few minutes away. The walk to the Vatican will help to build your appetite for a nice lunch or dinner (see *Cheap Eats in Italy* for suggestions in the area).

English Spoken: Yes

Facilities & Services: Air-conditioning (L20,000 extra), bar, direct-dial phones, some hair dryers, lift, mini-bars, radios, TVs

Nearest Tourist Attractions: Vatican, Tiber

VIA VENETO

Hotel Alexandra ★★★
Via Veneto, 18

AREA
Via Veneto
TELEPHONE
(06) 488.19.43/4/5
FAX
(06) 478.18.04
TELEX
622655 alex rmi
NUMBER OF ROOMS
45; all w/BST
CREDIT CARDS
AMEX, DC, MC, V
RATES
Single L160,000; double
L225,000; triple L265,000;
suite rates on request; breakfast
L14,000 per person extra

Although it lost some of its charm with modernization, the Alexandra is a Roman hotel that has managed to retain some style while yielding to the demand for color television, air-conditioned rooms, and mini-bars. It is located on the busy Via Veneto, just down from the American Embassy. Ear-shattering automobile and motor-scooter traffic and partying people in search of *la dolce vita* surge along this famous street 24 hours a day. If undisturbed sleep is a priority, it is best to request a room away from all the constant noise.

The comfortable rooms have enough space for guests to spread out and stay a while. The five suites, some with Art Deco furnishings, have nice bathrooms, with terry cloth towels and decent showers but, alas, no curtains. Room No. 36 has brass beds, Oriental rugs on the floors, a marble dresser, a large mirrored armoire, and a 1920s-style chandelier. Breakfast is a significant extra, so it might be smarter to eat elsewhere and put those lire toward a nice lunch or dinner. See *Cheap Eats in Italy* for loads of suggestions.

English Spoken: Yes

Facilities & Services: Air-conditioning, bar, direct-dial phones, mini-bars, lift, TVs, laundry service; buses stop in front of hotel, subway for Vatican next door

Nearest Tourist Attractions: Via Veneto and good nightlife, 20-minute walk to Coliseum and Piazza Venezia

Hotel Oxford ★★★
Via Boncompagni, 89

For someone wanting a well-located pleasant hotel with all the amenities, the Hotel Oxford fits the bill to a T. For night owls, the Via Veneto is close by, and for exercise enthusiasts, the Borghese Gardens is the perfect setting for an early-morning walk or jog. If you arrive by train, the cab ride will be about 10 to 15 minutes, depending on traffic.

Several sitting areas offer comfortable places to relax after a day of fitting in the "must-dos" of Rome. The well-lighted formal dining room serves a Continental breakfast and dinner. The breakfast is included with the room, but dinner is extra. The food is perfectly adequate, but hardly gourmet. It can be a port in a storm, however, if you are traveling with children or too tired to go out to eat in the evening. None of the rooms are decorator perfect, but all are clean and have good beds, serviceable bathrooms, and enough closet space. The hotel is on the American Embassy list for its personnel coming to Rome, so reservations can be tight if you wait until the last minute to make your plans.

English Spoken: Yes

Facilities & Services: Air-conditioning, bar, direct-dial phones, mini-bars, lift, private safes available, restaurant for dinner, radios, TVs

Nearest Tourist Attractions: Via Veneto, Borghese Gardens

AREA
Via Veneto and Borghese Gardens

TELEPHONE
(06) 482.89.52

FAX
(06) 481.53.49

TELEX
6303921

NUMBER OF ROOMS
58; all w/BST

CREDIT CARDS
AMEX, DC, MC, V

RATES
Single L160,000; double L220,000; triple L260,000; lower off-season rates; breakfast included

Hotel Pensione Merano ★★
Via Vittorio Veneto, 155

AREA
Via Veneto

TELEPHONE
(06) 482.17.96, 482.18.08, or
482.18.09

FAX
(06) 482.18.10

TELEX
None

NUMBER OF ROOMS
30; all w/BST

CREDIT CARDS
AMEX, DC, MC, V

RATES
Single L90,000; double
L130,000; triple L165,000;
breakfast included

Noise? Yes, unless you get a room on the back of the hotel. Rooms? About a B. No two are alike, and the furniture ranges from Garage Sale Gothic to almost-antique. Bathrooms? Above average, with stall showers and only a few indications of water damage. Location? Could not be better: right on Via Veneto, that famed Roman boulevard where people wear sunglasses regardless of the time of day or weather conditions and gather in the outdoor *caffès* hoping a little *la dolce vita* will rub off on them. Management? Pleasant and English-speaking. Bottom line? Well priced for this expensive area.

English Spoken: Yes

Facilities & Services: Bar, direct-dial phones, lift to 4th-floor reception but not to rooms

Nearest Tourist Attractions: Via Veneto, Borghese Gardens, Spanish Steps, good shopping

La Residenza ★★★
Via Emilia, 22–24

AREA
Via Veneto, Villa Borghese

TELEPHONE
(06) 488.07.89; toll-free from
U.S.: 1-800-448-8355

FAX
(06) 485.721

TELEX
410423 Giotel-I

NUMBER OF ROOMS
27; all w/BST

CREDIT CARDS
MC, V

RATES
Single L120,000;
double L215,000–245,000;
extra bed and breakfast
L85,000; children 2 and under
free; 10% discounts November
1–March 1; full American
buffet breakfast included

La Residenza is not cheap, but it is a polished, relaxed, and quiet converted villa in the high-rent district near Via Veneto and Villa Borghese. Its intimate clublike atmosphere, combined with the amenities of a luxury hotel and the comforts of a private home, make this a top choice for a stopover in the Eternal City.

The public rooms are outfitted with Oriental carpets, oil paintings, and overstuffed chairs and sofas. A copious American-style buffet breakfast includes everything from orange juice, fresh fruit, and cereals to yogurt, cheese, and bacon and eggs. The spacious bedrooms are covered in grass cloth and are comfortably furnished. Some have covered terraces, a real bonus during the hot summer months. The baths have good shelf space, terry cloth robes, heated towel racks, and large mirrors. The only room to avoid is No. 34, a windowless single that is horribly stuffy and hot anytime of the year. For those seeking nocturnal pleasures, the neighborhood has many famous nightclubs, but don't expect them to be in the budget category.

English Spoken: Yes

Facilities & Services: Air-conditioning, bar, direct-dial phones, hair dryers, mini-bars, lift, parking, satellite TVs, radios, in-house films

Nearest Tourist Attractions: Villa Borghese, Via Veneto

OTHER OPTIONS

CAMPING

Yes, you can camp in Rome. You can rent tents, but you will have to bring your own camp stove. Both these locations are on the far outskirts of the city and require long rides to get into central Rome. Prices are just about as cheap as you will find, so for some the savings may be worth the long trek to civilization.

Nomentano
Via Nomentano
Telephone: (06) 610.02.96

Open from Easter until October 1. Advance reservations are not necessary. Prices start at L8,500 per person in a tent. The tent space is L4,000.

Roma Camping
Five miles east of Rome off Aurelia Consular Road
Tel: (06) 623.018

Prices start at L8,000 per person in a tent or trailer.

HOLY HOTELS

Convents, monasteries, and religious institutions provide Spartan accommodations to travelers who do not mind austere surroundings (with a few exceptions), out-of-the-way locations (again with exceptions), and lockouts by 11 P.M. Of course, prices are generally low, in some lodgings meals are served, and it certainly is safe. Making arrangements by mail can be frustrating, however. Many simply do not answer because they are too busy. Showing up on the spot is not recommended either. Your best bet is to telephone for your reservations as far in advance as possible. Some English is usually spoken, but of course Italian will get you much farther. Mentioning your priest or bishop won't hurt either.

The following list is just to get you started.

Protezione della Giovane
Via Urbana, 158
Tel: (06) 460.056

Contact this organization in Rome to help you make arrangements.

Centro Assistenza Pastorale
Piazza Pio XII, 3
Tel: 698.49.34, 698.48.25, or 698.50.36

Write to them for a list of religious institutions in Rome that accept overnight guests.

Casa di Santa Brigida
Piazza Farnese, 96
Tel: (06) 686.57.21 or 685.53.70

Definitely the most central, and one of the best I found. Run by foreign nuns, it has the atmosphere of an elegant and aristocratic home. Meals are served, and reservations are required as far in advance as possible. Cash only. Prices start at L80,000 per person, including breakfast. To reserve, call them. They told me they don't have time to answer letters.

The Franciscan Sisters of the Atonement
Via Monte de Gallo, 105
Tel: (06) 630.78.20

Near Vatican City. Prices start at L30,000 per person, including breakfast. The pensione plan starts at L50,000 per person. There is a 10 P.M. curfew.

Fraterna Domus
Via dell Cancello, 9
Tel: (06) 654.27.27

Located between the Tiber and Piazza Navona. The 15 rooms cost L50,000 per person, with three meals included. Spartan, but clean and pleasant. The food is very good. Lockout is at 11 P.M.

Suore di Sant'Anna
Piazza Madonna dei Monti, 3
No telephone

The rooms are simple but clean. The rates start at L30,000 per person with breakfast, or L55,000 for three meals and the room. Lockout is at 11 P.M.

Suore Dorotee
Via del Gianicolo, 4
Tel: (06) 654.20.54 or 654.33.49

Halfway up Janiculum Hill above Vatican City, in a quiet spot with a pretty garden. Near the North American College, where many Americans study for the priesthood. Curfew is at 10:30 P.M.; a few rooms have private baths. They do not answer written requests. Prices start at L30,000 per person with breakfast.

Suore Teatine
Salita Monte del Gallo, 25
Tel: (06) 637.40.84 or 637.46.53

A room and breakfast costs L36,000 per person; the pensione plan with three meals is L57,000 per person. Curfew is at 11 P.M.

RESIDENCE HOTELS AND APARTMENTS

The advantages of an apartment stay are many. Generally, the prices go down the longer you stay. There will always be more room to spread out than in a hotel room, and with a kitchen you will save money by eating some meals in. Soon you will be living like a local, shopping with your neighbors and having your cappuccino every morning at the same bar, buying bread from the same baker, and fruit from your favorite stall in the open market.

International Services Apartment and Villa Rentals
Via Propaganda, 27, 0187 Rome, Italy

TELEPHONE
(06) 684.09.41/2
FAX
(06) 684.09.43
TELEX
None
CREDIT CARDS
None
RATES
Depends on type of rental

When planning a trip, often it is more important to know ahead of time about the pitfalls and problems that can otherwise ruin a dream vacation. If you only get one valuable piece of advice from *Cheap Sleeps in Italy*, I hope it will be *never* to use International Services, a real estate company that leases apartments and villas throughout Italy. I dealt with this company exclusively on my last trip to Italy. Up front they are helpful and promise everything from their offices in the United States and their headquarters in Rome. In reality, they deliver very little except massive headaches for their clients. Upon the client's arrival, they exit the job and leave the client alone to deal with the Italian landlords, many of whom do not speak English or, worse yet, are unavailable for anything except collecting your money in advance. You could be faced with freezing cold or boiling hot flats located up shadowy stairways and behind creaking doors, where nothing works except you, trying to open and shut windows, operate ancient plumbing, and keep the wiring from blowing up. In addition, you may find no sheets, towels, or maid service as agreed upon, as well as filthy quarters with the owner's dirty clothes, trash, and spoiled food sitting around. On top of this you will be charged hefty deposits and then, when asking about the return of the deposit after the agreed-upon waiting period, get nothing but returned letters and refused phone calls, and finally have to resort to legal action. This is an international service creating a nightmare no one needs, least of all you. Avoid them, *please*.

English Spoken: Yes
Facilities & Services: Varies with each rental

Mayfair Residence
Via Divills, 183

AREA
Via Veneto

Via Vittorio Veneto is one of Rome's most fashionable and expensive addresses, as well as the location of some of its grandest hotels. The Mayfair Residence is not one of them, but its position only a few minutes away from this tree-lined boulevard gives it a head start. Actually the Mayfair Residence is an apartment hotel offering impressively ritzy studios and one- and two-bedroom accommodations to those who are staying longer in Rome and need more space and amenities than normal hotel rooms provide. All the quarters have private terraces, exceptional furniture, and more closet space than many of us have in our own homes. The kitchens are well stocked, but if you are not up to preparing your own breakfast, there is a dining room where a Continental breakfast is served. As with other residence hotels, the longer the stay, the better the rate.

English Spoken: Yes

Facilities & Services: Air-conditioning, direct-dial phones, hair dryers, lift, fully equipped kitchens, private safes, TVs, maid service Mon–Sat

Nearest Tourist Attractions: Via Veneto, Villa Borghese Gardens

TELEPHONE
(06) 482.04.81 or 481.48.87

FAX
(06) 481.57.53

TELEX
None

NUMBER OF ROOMS
40 apartments; all w/BST

CREDIT CARDS
AMEX, DC, MC, V

RATES
Single L225,000; double L275,000; 3 or 4 persons L325,000; can stay 1 day or 1 year, with special rates for long stays; breakfast included

Palazzo al Velabro
Via del Velabro, 16

For first-timers it is not easy to find, but once there you will agree that the accommodations are exceptional. The Palazzo al Velabro sits on the Piazza Bocca della Verità, facing the Palentino Hill, the Arc of Giano, and the Temple of Vesta. The beautifully appointed and comfortable studios and apartments have modern furnishings, kitchens large enough for some serious cooking, excellent closet space, and enviable bathrooms with sink space, enclosed showers and tubs, and plenty of towels. The drawbacks are that the first and second floors have limited views and that the residence is quite a walk from shops, an important point if you are setting up housekeeping for any length of time. However, if you have a car, this won't be a problem—only the hairy Rome traffic will be. There also is good bus service across the Tiber to Trastevere, where there are many shops.

AREA
Across Tiber from Trastevere

TELEPHONE
(06) 679.27.58, 679.29.85 or 679.34.50

FAX
(06) 679.37.90

TELEX
None

NUMBER OF ROOMS
40 apartments; all w/BST

CREDIT CARDS
AMEX, DC

RATES
Studio for 1 or 2 persons L160,000 plus 9% tax; largest apartment for 3 or 4 persons L290,000 plus 9% tax; minimum stay 7 nights; lower rates for monthly stays; breakfast L12,000 extra

English Spoken: Yes

Facilities & Services: Air-conditioning, direct-dial phones, hair dryers, lift, fully outfitted kitchens, free parking in front, laundry service available, radios, TVs

Nearest Tourist Attractions: Coliseum, Forum, Trastevere, Tiber

Residenza di Ripetta
Via di Ripetta, 231

AREA
Piazza del Popolo

TELEPHONE
(06) 672.141

FAX
(06) 360.39.59

TELEX
630062 RIPETT

NUMBER OF ROOMS
70 studios and apartments; all w/BST

CREDIT CARDS
AMEX, DC, MC, V

RATES
Prices start at L1,400,000 per week, plus 9% tax; the longer the stay, the lower the rates; deposit required for all reservations

Some lucky travelers require a home base for a month or more, and hotel rooms can grow very small and impersonal over a long stay. Private rentals require (almost) a legal team in back of you to deal with all the red tape, nonfunctioning plumbing, and escalating costs you are guaranteed to encounter if you rent from an individual. The best choice for a long stay, in my opinion, is a residence hotel. At first glance it may seem expensive, but when you consider that you have the space and comfort of an apartment plus maid service, kitchens, parking, and other perks, it is worth the extra outlay, especially if a family or a group of three or four are involved. When you cost it out per person, it is not much more than a good hotel.

The Residenza di Ripetta, a former 17th-century convent near the Piazza del Popolo, offers exceptional apartments that vary in size from studios to two-level units. Every extra imaginable is offered, including a roof garden, a cocktail bar, and meeting rooms. The furnishings are modern, the closets tremendous, and the bathrooms well lighted, with shelf space and good towels. Many outstanding restaurants are close (see *Cheap Eats in Italy*), and you will be within walking distance of the best shopping in Rome.

English Spoken: Yes

Facilities & Services: Air-conditioning, bar, snack bar, direct-dial phones, fully outfitted kitchens, lift, meeting rooms, safe in each unit, radios, TVs

Nearest Tourist Attractions: Piazza del Popolo, shopping

Residence in Trastevere
Vicolo Moroni, 35–36–37–39 (Piazza Trilussa)

If you are traveling with a family, or if you are planning a long stay in Rome and want the independence of apartment living without the ulcer-producing hassle of renting from an individual, a residence hotel is *the* answer.

This residence hotel is in a picturesque corner of Trastevere, where laundry dries from the windows of ancient buildings, children play in the streets, elderly black-garbed widows gossip on corners on their way to market, and men gather in neighborhood bars to talk sports and politics. The apartments are some of the most charming you will find, with whitewashed walls, beamed ceilings, country furniture, nicely tiled floors, and every convenience except an elevator. Maid service, weekly linen changes, fully equipped kitchens, private safes, direct-dial phones, and remote-controlled televisions come with each unit. The office has very limited operating hours, from 9:30 A.M. to 1:30 P.M. Monday through Friday only. Saturday, Sunday, and afternoons it is shut tight, which could present a problem if something went wrong in your apartment. But—this is not enough of a drawback to prevent you from seriously considering one of the more appealing residence hotels I found in Rome.

English Spoken: Yes

Facilities & Services: Fully equipped apartments with air-conditioning in some, direct-dial phones, kitchens, private safes, TVs

Nearest Tourist Attractions: Trastevere

AREA
Trastevere

TELEPHONE
(06) 808.33.75

FAX
(06) 581.27.68

TELEX
None

NUMBER OF ROOMS
20 apartments; all w/BST

CREDIT CARDS
None!

RATES
L125,000–260,000 per day, including tax; rates depend on size of unit and number of occupants

STUDENT ACCOMMODATIONS

Listed below are only some of the low-cost housing possibilities available to students visiting Rome. It is important to realize that most of these facilities are open to visitors *only* when the regular students are away on vacation in the summer months and during some of the other vacation periods of the year. The accommodations are far from luxurious. Most of them are beds in dormitory rooms that sleep anywhere from two to ten people. You should plan on providing your own soap and towels. Usually sheets and blankets are available for a nominal fee. Many sites are far from the action in Rome, but the prices are right and bus service is usually quite reliable. *Always* call ahead to see if there is space before making any long treks.

Note: An International Youth Hostel Federation membership opens the door to inexpensive dorm-style accommodations in youth hostels worldwide. The IYHF membership costs $20 per year and is available from American Youth Hostels, P.O. Box 37613, Washington, D.C., 20013-7613; telephone (202) 783-6161.

Casa dello Studente
Via Cesare de Lollis, 24

Area: Città Universitaria
Telephone: (06) 490.243
Fax: None
Telex: None
Number of Rooms: 1,000 beds; all w/BST
Credit Cards: None
Rates: About $15 per night for a dormitory room; open from July 21–Sept 20; breakfast extra
English Spoken: Usually
Facilities & Services: Cafeteria-style dining room open to nonstudents, complete sports facilities nearby, no curfew
Nearest Tourist Attractions: Public transportation necessary

Centro Universitario Marianum
Via Matteo Boiardo, 30

Area: Outside of Rome
Telephone: (06) 700.54.53
Fax: None
Telex: None
Number of Rooms: 96; w/BST, 4; w/o BST, 92; half with shower & basin, half with basin only
Credit Cards: None
Rates: Single L30,000–35,000 or L55,000 per

person for 3 meals and room; double L55,000–
60,000 or L100,000 for 2, including meals; closed in
August; special rates for groups; breakfast L5,000
   English Spoken: Yes
   Facilities & Services: Lift, chapel, open 6:30 A.M.–
midnight, lockout at midnight, TV & VCR in
lounge, dining room for all meals
   Nearest Tourist Attractions: 20 minutes from
Coliseum, 10 minutes by bus from center of Rome

International Youth Hostel (Ostello del Foro Italico)
Via delle Olimpiadi, 61
   Area: Fringes of Rome
   Telephone: (06) 396.47.09 or 396.00.09
   Fax: None
   Telex: None
   Number of Rooms: 350 beds; w/BST, none; w/o
BST, all
   Credit Cards: None
   Rates: Single $15 per night per person; breakfast
included
   English Spoken: Yes
   Facilities & Services: Dorm-style rooms with
metal beds, showers included in price of room, guests
may stay only 3 nights, open 2–11 P.M., lockout at
9 A.M. with no room use during day
   Nearest Tourist Attractions: *Far* from center of
Rome
   Miscellaneous: For further information or
reservations, contact AIG, Via Carlo Poma, 2, Rome;
telephone: (06) 359.92.95

San Lorenzo Youth Center
Via Pfeiffer, 24 (off Via della Conciliazione)
   Telephone: (06) 698.53.32
   Open: 11 A.M.–7 P.M. daily
   The purpose of this Catholic youth center is to
enable young people from around the world to meet
one another, talk about their faith, and participate in
services in the chapel. In addition to the religious
aspect of the organization, the center provides

information about Rome, acquires tickets for papal audiences, and helps young people with places to stay—chiefly in pensiones and religious retreats. There is no charge for any of their services. The young, multilingual international staff is welcoming and delightful.

University Housing
Tourist Office at the train station or
Via Parigi, 5
Tel: (06) 463.748

The Italian Youth Hostel organization (AIG) runs a program with various universities in Rome to provide housing for tourists from July through September when the regular students are not occupying the dormitories. This program is open to any person. There is a one-week maximum stay, and the cost is around L25,000 per person per day including breakfast. For complete information on each location, contact one of the offices above.

YWCA
Via Cesare Balbo, 4

Area: Train Station
Telephone: (06) 460.460
Fax: None
Telex: None
Number of Rooms: 41; w/BST, none; w/o BST, all
Credit Cards: None
Rates: Single L38,500; double L32,000 per person; triple or quad L25,000 per person; breakfast included Mon–Sat
English Spoken: Limited
Facilities & Services: Always open, showers included in price of room, lockout at midnight, accepts women and married couples only, lunch served Mon–Sat 1–2:15 P.M., for L20,000
Nearest Tourist Attractions: Well located

VENICE

Venice cannot be learned by rote; it is absorbed through the pores.
— Anonymous

The same grandeur that inspired Byron, Goethe, Shelley, and Wagner is visible to the millions of visitors who come to Venice each year, making tourism her biggest industry by spending over $100 million per year. The Doge's Palace, St. Mark's Square, the Basilica, and the Bridge of Sighs recall the golden age of Venice, when Marco Polo sailed from the harbor to open trade routes to the East. Venice then rose to become Europe's main trading post between East and West. At its height, more than 200,000 people lived in Venice, three times its present population.

Venice is made up of 100 islands separated by more than 150 canals and joined by 400 bridges. It is divided into six districts, or *sestieri*: Castello, San Marco, and Canneregio on one side of the Grand Canal, and San Polo, Dorsoduro, and Santa Croce on the other. To know and understand Venice, it is essential that you arm yourself with the best street map money can buy, while still being prepared to become hopelessly lost in the magical beauty of this fairy tale city of gondolas and ornate palaces. Within each *sestiere* there is one long series of addresses, which are usually given by the *sestiere* and the number of the address (San Marco, 2202). Unless you are a native, chances are you will have no idea where that number is in the district of San Marco. To help you find addresses more easily, *Cheap Sleeps in Italy* lists the street, the number, and the *sestiere* (SS. Apostoli, 435, Cannaregio).

There is no use pretending that Venice is anything but a *very* expensive city to visit. However, time spent here does not call for dipping into retirement funds or mortgaging the ranch, although you will have to use a degree of self-restraint and, at the same time, plan on spending more for everything here than elsewhere in Italy. The best time to go is from mid-March to November. From the beginning of January until Carnevale, many hotels and shops close completely. However, in the off season, the pace is slower, the crowds are thin, and most of the hotel rates are significantly lower. Carnevale, which takes place during the two weeks leading up to Lent, and the two weeks around Christmas are traditionally overcrowded times that the average tourist should avoid.

Some hotels in Venice could have a higher rating, except that they are in historic buildings that cannot be altered with improvements such as elevators. You may sacrifice some comfort in a small bathroom that will never be modernized, but you will be compensated by the beauty of the frescoed ceilings and the age-old building surrounding you—and perhaps an unforgettable view of the Grand Canal.

USEFUL INFORMATION

Emergencies	114
Hospital Ospedale Civile	520.56.22
Medical assistance	520.08.25
Late-night pharmacy	192
Boat ambulance	523.00.00
Airport inquiries	661.111
Train inquiries	715.555
Consulate offices	GREAT BRITAIN: Palazzo Querini, 1051, Dorsoduro; 830.143 UNITED STATES: The closest U.S. representative is in Trieste at Via dei Pellegrini, 42; 040.19.17.80
Currency Exchange	Banca Cattolica del Veneto, Calle Goldoni, 4481, San Marco; 957.066; American Express, Salizzada S. Moisè, 1471, San Marco; 520.08.44
Telephone code for Venice	041

HOTELS IN VENICE BY *SESTIERE* (DISTRICT)

CANNAREGIO

Albergo Adua ★
Lista di Spagna, 233A

The hotel may be short on charm, but the reception is warm, which is more than can be said for some other hotels in the vicinity. After walking up two long flights of stairs from the busy street below, you will be greeted by Lucia Stefani, who has run this hotel for 16 years. The rooms have unimaginative modern furniture, and the floors are covered in red indoor-outdoor carpeting. Pretty floral wallpaper helps to break the monotony. Some rooms look onto blank walls, but others have a tiny balcony facing the street. The housekeeping is generally on its toes, and everything is shipshape in the rooms and hall facilities.

English Spoken: Yes
Facilities & Services: None
Nearest Tourist Attractions: Grand Canal, train station

AREA
Cannaregio
TELEPHONE
(041) 716.184
FAX
None
TELEX
None
NUMBER OF ROOMS
18; w/BST, 4; w/o BST 14
CREDIT CARDS
AMEX, DC, MC, V
RATES
Single L40,000;
double L50,000–80,000;
triple L70,000–100,000;
breakfast L8,000 extra

Albergo Bernardi-Semenzato ★
Calle del Oca, SS. Apostoli 4363–66

Ok, so it sags here and there, and you will see some peeling paint. You will also notice that the furniture could use a good refinishing, but devotees of this outpost for the down-and-out do not care about esthetics. They love the location near friendly bars and good low-cost restaurants (see *Cheap Eats in Italy*). They also like the outgoing owner, Maria Teresa Pepoli, who speaks perfect English and is loaded with money-saving hints and tips about what to see and do in Venice. The rooms on the first floor have showers, but those on the second and third do not. They are, however, much brighter. When looking at the bottom line, it isn't any great shakes, but it certainly is a Cheap Sleep in Venice that will be hard to beat.

AREA
Cannaregio
TELEPHONE
(041) 522.72.57
FAX
None
TELEX
None
NUMBER OF ROOMS
18; w/BST, 7; w/o BST, 11
CREDIT CARDS
V
RATES
Single L30,000–35,000;
double L45,000–65,000; triple
L65,000–75,000; quad
L75,000–85,000; breakfast
L3,500 extra

English Spoken: Yes

Facilities & Services: None; 1 A.M. curfew

Nearest Tourist Attractions: Ghetto, Rialto Bridge, Grand Canal

Albergo S. Lucia ★
Calle Misericordia, 358

AREA
Cannaregio

TELEPHONE
(041) 715.180

FAX
None

TELEX
None

NUMBER OF ROOMS
15; w/BST, 5; w/o BST, 10

CREDIT CARDS
MC, V

RATES
Single L50,000; double L70,000–100,000; triple L90,000–125,000; quad L155,000; breakfast included, but can be deducted (L8,000) in off seasons

No carpets, no charm, but a pretty, sunny front patio, spotlessly clean rooms, and stall showers *with* doors more than make up for the lack of zing in the rooms. The hotel is located on a peaceful side street near the "zoo" area along Lista de Spagna, which runs from the train station. The rooms are all good sized, light, and quiet, ensuring visitors a peaceful night's rest. Breakfast can be served inside in a tiny breakfast room with four tables, or on the front patio, which is shielded from the street and pedestrians by an ivy-covered fence bordered by flower beds. The breakfast is mandatory during the high season, but in the winter, the cost can be deducted from the room rate.

English Spoken: Yes

Facilities & Services: None

Nearest Tourist Attractions: Train station, Grand Canal

Hotel Abbazia ★★★
Calle Priuli, 66

AREA
Cannaregio

TELEPHONE
(041) 717.333

FAX
(041) 717.949

TELEX
None

NUMBER OF ROOMS
39; all w/BST

CREDIT CARDS
AMEX, DC, MC, V

In its golden age 120 years ago, the Abbazia was a Franciscan monastery with 40 or 50 monks filling the rooms. Their work included producing a special medicinal water, but now the main center for this production has been moved to Verona. About ten years ago, the friars sold part of the property, and it was converted into this tranquil hotel. Today a few of the monks still live in quarters on the other side of the garden and run the church next to the train station.

The location, in a small alley next to a row of low-cost hotels behind the station, is not spectacular in itself. However, once inside the hotel, this approach will soon be forgotten, and you will feel a million miles removed from all the activity surrounding the station. The rooms have been faithfully restored, keeping the quiet atmosphere and spirit of the original monastery always in mind. Scattered throughout the hotel are pieces of furniture the monks used in their daily lives and church services. For example, the lobby has wooden abbey benches around the perimeter, and the breakfast room with a huge skylight was once the kitchen. The largest rooms are upstairs and face the garden, which was the central courtyard of the monastery. All have plenty of closet and luggage space, good light, nice bathrooms, and attractive repro-duction furnishings.

Note: The management offers significant discounts to Cheap Sleep readers who mention the book when reserving and present it upon check-in.

English Spoken: Yes

Facilities & Services: Air-conditioning, bar, direct-dial phones, hair dryers, mini-bars, TVs

Nearest Tourist Attractions: Grand Canal, train station

Hotel al Gobbo ★
Campo S. Geremia, 312

Maria di Vinco fits everyone's picture of the perfect Italian grandmother: regal, yet genteel and with a heart of gold. She does not speak English, but her grandson does, so you won't have communication problems as long as he is around. The hotel is named after the original owner; the word *gobbo* means "hunchback." The Italians have a superstition that if you touch the back of someone with a hump, it will bring you good luck. If you stay here, you will feel that you have had good luck with your hotel selection, because for a one-star, it is a brilliant choice. The neat bedrooms have unadorned wash-and-wipe furniture. None have private toilets, but plans are in the works to add some. A few of the roosts overlook a lovely garden and others open onto a square. Breakfast is served on a round table in the communal sitting room where you will feel as though you are in someone's nice home, not in a hotel near the train station in Venice.

RATES
Off Seasons (Jan–Mar and Dec): Single L60,000–90,000; double L105,000; triple L140,000; quad L180,000. *High Seasons (Apr–June, Sept–Nov):* Single L70,000; double L105,000–140,000; triple L180,000; quad L220,000. *Mid-season (July and Aug):* Single L70,000–105,000; double L120,000; triple L160,000; quad L200,000. Breakfast included

AREA
Cannaregio

TELEPHONE
(041) 715.001

FAX
None

TELEX
None

NUMBER OF ROOMS
11; w/BST, 5 with shower only; none with toilet

CREDIT CARDS
MC, V

RATES
Single L45,000; double L65,000–70,000; triple L80,000; breakfast included

English Spoken: Yes, most of the time

Facilities & Services: Lockout at 2 A.M.

Nearest Tourist Attractions: Train station, Ghetto, Grand Canal

Hotel Hesperia ★★
Calle Riello, 459

AREA
Cannaregio

TELEPHONE
39 – (041) 715.251

FAX
(041) 715.112

TELEX
None

NUMBER OF ROOMS
20; w/BST, 18; w/o BST, 2

CREDIT CARDS
AMEX, MC, V

RATES
Single L95,000; double L140,000; triple L190,000; breakfast included; lunch or dinner L33,000

Massimiliano Bico's Hotel Hesperia is a nice hideaway for romantics who do not like big, brassy hotels in busy areas. Frankly, it is just the sort of hotel most people are hoping to find, and when they do, whisper its name only to a select few for fear of ruining it for themselves. If you are willing to go just beyond the well-worn tourist track of hotels near the train station, you will be rewarded by an outstanding two-star that offers many three-star features, as well as an excellent gourmet restaurant, Il Melograno (see *Cheap Eats in Italy*, page 108). This tranquil haven on a quiet little canal is a fully renovated townhouse with the aura of a warm Italian home. Each room is named after a well-known artist, and a copy of one of the artist's works hangs inside. The restful bedrooms are not large, but they are beautifully equipped and tastefully decorated in shades of blue with Murano glass chandeliers and superb bathrooms. Signor Bico and his staff do everything they can to provide a warm welcome and fine service to their guests. After a stay here, I am sure you will join the many who adore this wonderful small hotel in Venice.

English Spoken: Yes

Facilities & Services: Bar, direct-dial phones, hair dryers, mini-bars, private room safes, restaurant, TVs

Nearest Tourist Attractions: Must use vaporettos near train station, about a 10-minute walk

Hotel Mignon ★★
SS. Apostoli, 4532

AREA
Cannaregio

TELEPHONE
(041) 523.73.88

FAX
(041) 520.8658

If you can ignore the routinely serviceable lobby that has no warmth whatsoever, and concentrate instead on having a good night's sleep in a dynamite location between the Ca' d'Oro and the Rialto Bridge, you will be happy staying at the Mignon. The genial manager goes all out to be helpful to his guests. When I was there, he offered to have a friend help me move my things so I would not have to hire someone to do it for me.

The rooms are unquestionably small, uniformly plain, and not comfortable for long stays. If you ask for a room on the first or second floor, you will get a spic-and-span place to bunk for a few days, with either your own bathroom or the use of one down the hall. Several rooms have a nice view onto the back patio where summer breakfasts are served. If you check into a room on the third floor, you may be lucky and get one that has a terrace. Number 31 on this floor has not been upgraded, but there is no need to apologize because the terrace saves it. Prices are good for the area, especially if you are here during the winter and can take advantage of the 15 percent discount.

English Spoken: Yes

Facilities & Services: Fans in rooms

Nearest Tourist Attractions: Near Ca' d'Oro and Rialto Bridge

TELEX
None

NUMBER OF ROOMS
21; w/BST, 15; w/o BST, 6

CREDIT CARDS
MC, V

RATES
Single L57,000–86,000; double L81,000–117,000; triple L153,000; quad L189,000; breakfast included; 15% discount in winter; hotel closed Jan and half of Feb, depending on Carnevale

Hotel Minerva & Nettuno ★
Lista di Spagna, 230

The area around the train station in Venice is populated with scores of cheap one-star hotels, many of which are simply too grim to consider, no matter what the price. You can trust me on this, because during my stay in Venice, I think I looked at every one-star along the Lista di Spagna and the many side streets that lead off of it.

The Minerva & Nettuno is about a five-minute walk from the train station on the left side of Lista di Spagna. The reception area is on the ground level, with a dwarfish breakfast room and a closet-sized kitchen squeezed into a corner. The rest of the hotel is divided into two sections, one definitely preferable to the other. The one to *avoid* is the ten-room annex, which is usually reserved for groups of young people. The second and third floors of the new section are where you want to be. The front rooms face the

AREA
Cannaregio

TELEPHONE
(041) 715.968 or 524.23.66

FAX
(041) 524.2139

TELEX
None

NUMBER OF ROOMS
31; w/BST, 10; w/o BST, 21

CREDIT CARDS
MC, V

RATES
Single L40,000–55,000; double L55,000–85,000; triple L65,000–110,000; quad L80,000–125,000; breakfast L10,000 extra

street, and a few have their own balcony. Number 12 is a pretty room, actually much better than those in many two-stars in the neighborhood. It does not have a view, but the shower has a curtain, there is great space, frilly pink and white Murano glass chandeliers give good light, and tile floors with Oriental rugs keep it cooler when the weather sizzles. English is spoken, you are not obliged to pay for breakfast if you do not eat it, and the prices are in line for Venice.

English Spoken: Yes

Facilities & Services: Direct-dial phones in new section

Nearest Tourist Attractions: Close to train station and vaporetto stops with access to all of Venice

Hotel Rossi ★
Calle delle Procurate, 262

AREA
Cannaregio

TELEPHONE
(041) 715.164 or 717.784

FAX
None

TELEX
None

NUMBER OF ROOMS
14; w/BST, 5; w/o BST, 9

CREDIT CARDS
AMEX, MC, V

RATES
Single L45,000–60,000; double L60,000–90,000; triple L80,000–115,000; quad L95,000–140,000; breakfast included, but may be deducted in off seasons on request

The family-owned Hotel Rossi is a Cheap Sleep that may entail a few sacrifices if you choose to stay here. First of all, there is no elevator, but the climb up three flights of stairs is easy if you are in shape and do not have lung problems. Next, you will have to give up charm and character for nondescript modern furniture, chenille bedspreads, and some dreary outlooks. The good news is that the hotel staff is cheerful, the rooms are clean and kept up, and the plumbing works well. Another point in the hotel's favor is its location within walking distance of both the train station and Piazzale Roma parking garages. Its location also ensures quiet nights, because it is set off the busy Lista di Spagna on a narrow alley. The hotel is closed for all of January and February, and in the off seasons you may not be required to take breakfast, which is mandatory the rest of the year.

English Spoken: Yes

Facilities & Services: None

Nearest Tourist Attractions: Train station, Grand Canal, several vaporetto stops nearby

Hotel San Geremia ★
Campo San Geremia, 290A

Affordability is the thrust at the San Geremia, a clean choice especially suited to lone travelers. The main sitting room has a large picture window opening onto the Campo San Geremia and offers great moments in people-watching. Next to this is a dollhouse-size breakfast room with a miniature bar. To reach your room, you will have to cope with stairs and unfortunate green wallcovering in the halls, but you cannot fault the rooms even though they do have chenille and a few skyless vistas along the back. All rooms have direct-dial phones and color televisions, two amenities rarely found in one-star hotels. If you live on the front side, you will overlook the *Campo* in front, which is dotted with children playing and old people gossiping and feeding the pigeons. Other pluses include nice baths with shelf space, shower doors, and white terry cloth towels. The management speaks English, and you are close to vaporetto stops with access across the Grand Canal to St. Mark's Square and the Rialto Bridge. It all adds up to a good sleep at non-killer prices, and that is what all Cheap Sleepers want.

English Spoken: Yes

Facilities & Services: Bar, direct-dial phones, TVs

Nearest Tourist Attractions: Must use vaporettos; close to train station and parking for cars at Piazzale Roma

AREA
Cannaregio

TELEPHONE
(041) 716.245 or 716.260

FAX
None

TELEX
None

NUMBER OF ROOMS
21; w/BST, 14; w/o BST, 7

CREDIT CARDS
AMEX, DC, MC, V

RATES
Single L50,000–75,000; double L75,000–105,000; triple L140,000; quad L175,000; quint L200,000; breakfast included; discounts in off seasons; usually closed Dec 1–15

CASTELLO

Albergo Doni ★
Calle del Vin, 4656 (Riva Schiavoni, S. Zaccaria)

In back of St. Mark's Square as you head toward San Zaccaria is this exceptional Cheap Sleep. The rooms either overlook the parked gondolas on the Rio del Vin or a garden with fruit trees. Large and airy bedrooms outfitted with only a bidet and a basin with hot and cold running water tell you they have not been blessed by renovation. They are, nevertheless, spotless and always booked by an older group

AREA
Castello

TELEPHONE
(041) 522.42.67

FAX
None

TELEX
None

NUMBER OF ROOMS
11; all w/BST

CREDIT CARDS
None

RATES
Single L50,000; double L75,000; triple L100,000; quad L125,000; showers included, towels L1500 each; breakfast included, but can be deducted at L10,000 per person; hotel closed Dec 20–Mar 15

of Cheap Sleepers who know a bargain deal when they see one. To make your sleep here even cheaper, ask to have the 10,000-lire cost of breakfast deducted, and go instead to one of the neighborhood *caffès* and do as the Venetians do: have your cappuccino and *cornetto* while standing at the bar.

Note: The hotel is closed from December 20 to March 15.

English Spoken: Yes

Facilities & Services: None; 1 A.M. curfew

Nearest Tourist Attractions: St. Mark's Square, Grand Canal

Albergo Paganelli ★★
Campo S. Zaccaria, 4687

AREA
Castello

TELEPHONE
(041) 522.43.24

FAX
(041) 523.9267

TELEX
None

NUMBER OF ROOMS
23; w/BST, 20; w/o BST, 3

CREDIT CARDS
AMEX, MC, V

RATES
Single L88,000–95,000; double L100,000–135,000; triple L160,000–180,000; quad L220,000; breakfast included but may sometimes be deducted at L12,500

Most hotels along this premium stretch of water in Venice charge almost half again as much as the Paganelli. While the prices may be high for some committed Cheap Sleepers, there is significant value in what you get. Francesco Paganelli continues to carry on the family tradition of hotel-keeping that was started when his grandfather opened the hotel in 1874. Before that, the hotel was part of the San Zaccaria convent, whose claim to fame came in the 16th century when the nuns revolted against the bishop and the Church.

The hotel now consists of two buildings. One is the annex, which has recently been renovated. These rooms are certainly more up-to-date than the others, with full air-conditioning and new bathrooms. Frankly, I would recommend that you forego the few amenities in the annex and reserve a room in the older section, which has a stunning view of the lagoon just east of St. Mark's Square. These view rooms are *always* in great demand and are booked months in advance, so do not wait until the last minute to make your reservations.

English Spoken: Yes

Facilities & Services: Some rooms air-conditioned, direct-dial phones, some hair dryers

Nearest Tourist Attractions: St. Mark's Square

Hotel Fontana ★★
Campo S. Provolo, 4701

At the end of a long, cold, blustery day, I was in a hurry to hop on the vaporetto at the San Zaccaria landing stage and go back to my warm flat on Campo Squellini. I was not anxious to inspect another hotel, but when I passed the Hotel Fontana, I knew I had to go in and see it. I am glad I did, because it turned out to be a find, one of the best two-stars in the area. A warm family atmosphere prevails from the sitting room and bar throughout the four floors of the hotel. The well-lit, well-furnished rooms have shiny bathrooms, pleasing color schemes, and crisp cotton bedspreads. The majority have views over the garden or San Zaccaria church. I like Room No. 11 on the fourth floor because of its private terrace, which is pleasant for a summer breakfast or an afternoon drink. Families should request No. 14, a two-room suite with a skylight and a charming view of the church.

English Spoken: Yes

Facilities & Services: Bar, direct-dial phones, TV on request L10,000 per day

Nearest Tourist Attractions: St. Mark's Square

AREA
Castello

TELEPHONE
(041) 521.05.33 or 522.05.79

FAX
(041) 523.10.40

TELEX
None

NUMBER OF ROOMS
16; all w/BST

CREDIT CARDS
AMEX, MC, V

RATES
Single L90,000; double L122,000; triple L170,000; quad L210,000; lower off-season rates; breakfast included, but may be deducted on request at L15,000 per person

Hotel Locanda Remedio ★★
Calle del Remedio, 4412

To find the Locanda Remedio, walk four bridges down from the Bridge of Sighs, then across the Ponte Remedio, down Calle Remedio past the Hotel Atlantico, and take the first right down a dark lane to a tiny square where you will find this 14-room hotel. Only a year ago, this was a worn-out location that attracted cash-strapped aristocrats who like to camp. Now, all this has changed, thanks to a seven-month transformation project presided over by owner Gianni Scarpa. The enormous amount of work and effort made it into a lovely hotel befitting its former life as an inn where nobles came to drink and celebrate after being presented at the Doge's Palace.

For something special, ask for the room with the hand-painted ceiling or, if traveling family style, reserve the mezzanine. These three rooms used to be

AREA
Castello

TELEPHONE
(041) 520.62.32

FAX
(041) 521.04.85

TELEX
None

NUMBER OF ROOMS
14; w/BST, 10; w/o BST, 4

CREDIT CARDS
None

RATES
Single L80,000; double L90,000–125,000; lower off-season rates; breakfast L8,000 extra

the maid's quarters, but now can be blocked off for those wishing to stay together but not all in the same room. The hotel is nicely appointed with antiques and reproductions. The management is very accommodating and friendly, and the location is good for all the things a tourist wants to do in Venice.

English Spoken: Yes

Facilities & Services: Direct-dial phones, private room safes

Nearest Tourist Attractions: Within walking distance to St. Mark's Square and Rialto Bridge

Hotel Scandinavia ★★★
Campo di S. Maria Formosa, 5240

AREA
Castello

TELEPHONE
(041) 522.35.07; toll-free from U.S. 1-800-448-8355

FAX
None

TELEX
420359

NUMBER OF ROOMS
29; w/BST, 25; w/o BST, 4

CREDIT CARDS
AMEX, MC, V

RATES
Single L104,000–158,000; double L150,000–215,000; triple L290,000–365,000; discount in off seasons; breakfast included

Guests want to stay at the Hotel Scandinavia for its location on Campo di S. Maria Formosa, which is midway between the Rialto Bridge and St. Mark's Square. The hotel is furnished in elaborate 18th-century Venetian style. A marble staircase leads from the ground floor entrance and formal dining room to the first-floor reception and sitting room. This area is dominated by an ornate wooden ceiling and has no shortage of Murano glass windows, mirrors, and lights. Eight rooms face the square. Room No. 5 is the biggest and best in the house, even if it is a little overdone, with flowery wallpaper and green velvet bedspreads and drapes. Room No. 1 leads off the sitting area and has the same pretty ceiling and two windows opening onto the square. Prices are good for a three-star hotel, especially if you go in an off season and can take advantage of the discounted rates.

English Spoken: Yes

Facilities & Services: Air-conditioning at 10% of room rate per day, direct-dial phones, mini-bars, TVs at 10% of room rate

Nearest Tourist Attractions: Rialto Bridge, St. Mark's Square

La Residenza ★★
Campo Bandiera e Moro, 3608

AREA
Castello

The quiet neighborhood around the hotel is a world away from the milling hordes near St. Mark's

Square and the pedestrian-clogged Riva degli Schiavoni, both of which are only a short walk from the hotel. When you reach the Campo Bandiera e Moro and see the red flag flying in front of the building, and the colorful flower boxes under the windows, you will know you have found La Residenza. To enter, press the nose of the lion to the right of the large entrance doors, and walk through the courtyard and up two flights of stairs to the lobby and reception desk. This 15th-century Gothic structure was the former home of the Gritti family, one of the wealthiest, and certainly the most prestigious, in Venice. The ornate salon, with its magnificent sculpted plaster walls and ceilings, lovely paintings, marble floors and massive furniture, suggests the type of opulent life the former residents of the palazzo led. While not for everyone, the hotel is a long-enduring favorite among its many clients, thanks in a large part to the welcome of owner and manager Franco Tagliapietra, his dog Ugo, and his Ethiopian short-haired cat Salome, who happily sleeps anywhere she fancies in the salon. Although the 16 rooms do not compare with the ornate lobby, they do have some appealing antiques and all the modern accoutrements we deem necessary, such as color televisions, mini-bars, and private bathrooms in all but two.

English Spoken: Yes

Facilities & Services: Air-conditioning L10,000 extra per day, direct-dial phones, mini-bars, TVs

Nearest Tourist Attractions: St. Mark's Square

TELEPHONE
(041) 528.53.15

FAX
(041) 523.8859

TELEX
None

NUMBER OF ROOMS
16; w/BST, 14; w/o BST, 2

CREDIT CARDS
AMEX, DC, V

RATES
Single L85,000; double L105,000–130,000; triple L185,000; breakfast included

Locanda Toscana-Tofanelli (no stars)
Via Garibaldi, 1650

For a truly Spartan, no-frills Cheap Sleep in a hotel that has not been remodeled or upgraded since it opened decades ago, try the Locanda Toscana-Tofanelli. The seaside location is more than a few heartbeats away from the tourist thick of things, but the low prices and the sweet sisters who run it more than make up for these "inconveniences." Some people will consider the location fringe, but others

AREA
Castello

TELEPHONE
(041) 523.57.22

FAX
None

TELEX
None

NUMBER OF ROOMS
9; w/BST, none; w/o BST, all
CREDIT CARDS
None
RATES
Single L22,000–25,000;
double L42,000–45,000;
triple L65,000; hotel is closed
Nov–Jan; breakfast L5,000
extra

will enjoy walking along the nearby narrow canals, whose waters are bordered by buildings with flowers cascading from the windows, children and dogs happily playing in the street, and lines of laundry flapping overhead. The area is a photo opportunity if there ever was one. Actually, from this point you are about a 15-minute walk to St. Mark's, and there are vaporetto stops even closer.

The rooms are definitely *vintage*, with exposed pipes and bare floors, and some have no running water. Four or five rooms do have views, and three have little balconies that are perfect perches for people-watching. Naturally, all the facilities are the down-the-hall variety.

The sisters watch everything with an eagle eye and lock up tight at midnight after closing the restaurant they run in conjunction with the hotel (see *Cheap Eats in Italy*, page 113).

English Spoken: No

Facilities & Services: None

Nearest Tourist Attractions: Within a 15-minute walk

Nuovo Teson ★★
Ramo Pescaria, 3980 (off Riva degli Schiavoni)

AREA
Castello
TELEPHONE
(041) 522.99.29 or 520.55.55
FAX
(041) 528.53.35
TELEX
None
NUMBER OF ROOMS
30; all w/BST
CREDIT CARDS
AMEX, DC, MC, V
RATES
Single L92,000;
double L125,000; L39,000 for
extra person in room;
sometimes lower off-season
rates; breakfast included

The Nuovo Teson is set back on a pretty square just off the busy Riva degli Schiavoni. The rooms are modest in appointments, yet they offer plenty of space for daytime living. They are uniformly done in reproduction Venetian-style painted furniture, with only an occasional modern piece thrown in. Downstairs there is a cozy bar with inviting chairs and a sunny breakfast room overlooking the street. The hotel is just a whisper or two away from St. Mark's and close to some of the best restaurants I found in Venice (see *Cheap Eats in Italy*).

English Spoken: Yes

Facilities & Services: Bar, direct-dial phones, fans in rooms, radios

Nearest Tourist Attractions: St. Mark's Square

Pensione Bucintoro ★★
Riva San Biagio, 2135

The Bucintoro is an old hotel with a minimum of style, few upgrades, and no character. However, the fabulous views save it from oblivion. All the rooms have a view over the San Marco basin, with the Lido on one side and the Doge's Palace on the other. Another bonus is the dining room, which serves lunch and dinner daily. It is the answer for those voyagers who are too tired to venture out on their own, or for those traveling with small children. From this site, it is an easy walk to St. Mark's Square, the center of all the action in Venice. For trips farther afield, you can walk along the Riva degli Schiavoni and catch one of the vaporettos that depart every few minutes. If you are worried about the rooms, no need to. They are clean and neat, just boring—but remember the view!

English Spoken: Yes

Facilities & Services: Bar, direct-dial phones, room service, 1 A.M. curfew

Nearest Tourist Attractions: St. Mark's Square; close to vaporetto stops

AREA
Castello

TELEPHONE
(041) 522.32.40

FAX
(041) 523.52.24

TELEX
None

NUMBER OF ROOMS
28; w/BST, 23; w/o BST, 5

CREDIT CARDS
None; cash only

RATES
Single L55,000–70,000 (half-board L85,000–97,000); double L78,000–110,000 (half-board L68,000–85,000 per person); triple L145,000 (half-board L76,000 per person); lower off-season rates. Breakfast included

Pensione Casa Verardo ★
Calle Castagna, 4765, off Ruga Giuffa

On a little canal just after you cross over the Ponte Storto, you will see the Pensione Casa Verardo, a family-run site dear to the hearts of Cheap Sleepers. The building is a 14th-century palazzo that was at one time a school for Jewish students when the ghetto extended this far. The pensione has family furniture, knickknacks of dubious distinction, and a barking dog named Maxi. The rooms are huge, with high ceilings, tile floors, and a view to the buildings across the walkway. The airless cubicle showers were afterthoughts. If you do stay here, you should try to avoid Room No. 11, a single with no closet or running water, on the ground floor next to an air shaft and the public toilet. The other rooms in the hotel are okay; just remember this one and do not get it.

AREA
Castello

TELEPHONE
(041) 528.61.27

FAX
None

TELEX
None

NUMBER OF ROOMS
12; w/BST, 2; w/o BST, 10

CREDIT CARDS
MC, V

RATES
Single L40,000; double L70,000–80,000; triple L95,000–115,000; quad L115,000–135,000; breakfast L6,000 extra

English Spoken: Yes
Facilities & Services: Lift
Nearest Tourist Attractions: St. Mark's Square

DORSODURO

Agli Alboretti Hotel ★★
Rio Terrà Antonia Foscarini, Accademia 884

AREA
Dorsoduro

TELEPHONE
(041) 523.00.58

FAX
(041) 521.0128

TELEX
None

NUMBER OF ROOMS
25; w/BST, 20; w/o BST, 5

CREDIT CARDS
AMEX, MC, V

RATES
Single L95,000–116,000; double L160,000; triple L205,000; room, breakfast, and one other meal L115,000 per person; breakfast included and cannot be deducted

The Agli Alboretti, owned by Dina Linguerri and her daughter Anna, is close to the Accademia Gallery, which has the world's finest collection of Venetian art. For other sightseeing, the Accademia vaporetto stop is only a few steps from the hotel.

The entrance off the street leads to an intimate paneled lobby, with a collection of attractive oils and watercolors of Venice displayed on the walls. An interesting model of a 17th-century ship stands proudly in the window. Beyond the lobby is a little lounge, and a garden with a vine-covered arbor where you can have breakfast on warm mornings, or relax in the shade on hot summer afternoons. The rooms are all very small and so are the bathrooms, but this is an old building and one cannot expect spacious quarters. Number 7 has bright white walls, a heavily beamed ceiling, dark wood furniture, and a view to the street through a set of double windows. Number 5, with blue floral wallpaper, has antique walnut bedside stands, a small writing table, and two attractive chairs. Avoid Room No. 19; it is too small and dark for any degree of comfort. The Linguerris operate a high-end restaurant next door to their hotel and can arrange for half-board for lunch or dinner for guests.

English Spoken: Yes

Facilities & Services: Bar, direct-dial phones, dining room

Nearest Tourist Attractions: Accademia Gallery, Zattere, Gesuati Church, Guggenheim Collection

Antico Capon ★
Campo Santa Margherita, 3004B

AREA
Dorsoduro

When I stayed in Venice, my apartment was just off the Campo Santa Margherita, so I came to know the area well. Everything—well, almost everything—you will need or want is right here, from pizza, pastries, and a supermarket to locksmiths, hairdressers, and a laundry that does the most beautiful finish work I have ever seen. Most mornings the campo has stalls selling fruit, vegetables, and fresh fish. The best time to catch all the flavor is early on a Saturday morning when more stalls are set up. In late afternoon, the area serves as a playground for the neighborhood children and a meeting place for gossip and cappuccino for their mothers. All this brings me to the Antico Capon, a one-star wonder right on the square. The approach, up linoleum-covered stairs, is not inspiring, and neither are the green halls. Remember though, you are not living in these areas; it is the room that counts, and here they all do. For a one-star, the rooms are surprising: large and freshly painted, with decent furniture and acceptable bed coverings. Three overlook the campo and all the action, and four face the back. Everything is presided over by a sweet woman who does not speak English, but understands broken Italian beautifully.

English Spoken: No

Facilities & Services: None

Nearest Tourist Attractions: Campo Santa Margherita, within walking distance of Accademia Gallery; close to 2 vaporetto stops

TELEPHONE
(041) 528.52.92

FAX
None

TELEX
None

NUMBER OF ROOMS
7; w/BST, 5; w/o BST, 2

CREDIT CARDS
None

RATES
Single L40,000–65,000; double L55,000–85,000; showers L3,500

Hotel Pausania ★★★
Rio di San Barnaba, 2824

The Pausania is a paragon of tranquility and comfort near colorful San Barnaba Square and the last of the floating markets on a barge along the San Barnaba Canal. The overall effect of the hotel is pleasantly balanced, friendly, and agreeable. The lovely entry through the courtyard, with its original well and stairway, leads to a beamed lobby with leather sofas and Oriental rugs scattered on terrazzo floors. An inviting breakfast room opens onto a pretty garden. The neutrally done rooms are good-sized and have all the expected accessories: hair dryers, heated towel racks, mini-bars, and color televisions. Families

AREA
Dorsoduro

TELEPHONE
(041) 522.20.83

FAX
None

TELEX
420178 PAU V CE

NUMBER OF ROOMS
26; all w/BST

CREDIT CARDS
AMEX, MC, V

RATES
Single L155,000; double
L210,000; triple L270,000;
suite L330,000; breakfast
included

will like No. 306, the top-floor suite with a peekaboo window overlooking the tiled roofs and terraces of the neighboring homes. From the hotel door, guests are close to excellent restaurants (see *Cheap Eats in Italy*), interesting shops (see "Cheap Chic," page 159) and the Accademia vaporetto stop.

English Spoken: Yes

Facilities & Services: Air-conditioning, bar, direct-dial phones, hair dryers, mini-bars, TVs, radios

Nearest Tourist Attractions: Campo San Barnaba, Campo Santa Margherita, Accademia Gallery

Hotel Tivoli ★★
Ca' Foscari, 3838

AREA
Dorsoduro

TELEPHONE
(041) 523.77.52 or 522.26.56

FAX
(041) 22656

TELEX
None

NUMBER OF ROOMS
24; w/BST, 22; w/o BST, 2

CREDIT CARDS
AMEX, DC, MC, V

RATES
Single L60,000–90,000;
double L85,000–125,000;
triple L160,000; quad
L200,000; breakfast included
but may be deducted at
L15,000 per person

If you are in Venice during the ten days between Christmas and New Year's, you will not be able to stay at Gina Gardin's Hotel Tivoli because it will be closed. During the rest of the year, this smart two-star plays to a full house of contented regulars and visitors who have found it through word of mouth. The hotel offers exceptionally good value and comfort along with friendly service in one of the most interesting parts of Venice, near Campo Santa Margherita. If you are traveling with a family, ask for No. 34, a sunny triple with a sloped ceiling and a private terrace. If there are only two of you, No. 25, one of the best in the hotel, has high ceilings, tile floors, reproduction furniture, and a large bath with a shower. In most of the other rooms, the furnishings are the hose-down Formica type and the bedspreads are chenille, but they are well maintained and clean. The beamed dining room overlooking the garden is done in a country Italian theme with well-spaced large tables set with nice linens and china. To be a really Cheap Sleeper, ask to have the 15,000 lire for breakfast deducted from your bill and walk down the street to Tonolo, one of the best pastry shops in the area (see *Cheap Eats in Italy*, page 120). Here you can mingle with the packed crowd that arrives every morning for a cup of cappuccino and a melt-in-your-mouth breakfast goodie.

English Spoken: Yes
Facilities & Services: Direct-dial phones
Nearest Tourist Attractions: Campo Santa Margherita

Locanda Ca' Foscari ★
Calle della Frescada, 3887B

The hotel is located between Campo Santa Tomà and Campo Santa Barnaba, one of the most interesting areas of Venice. This is an upper-middle-class area, filled with people going about their daily lives. You will find many small shops, bakeries, bars, *caffès*, and restaurants, but few are geared specifically to the tourist trade.

During the school term at the nearby university, many students live at the hotel. Other foreign student groups often use the hotel from March through June. This does not take away from its nice family-run atmosphere. The rooms are well cared for and kept up on a regular maintenance schedule. The walls are covered halfway down with fabric and the rest with white paint. Each room is different, but they are coordinated and do not have sleazy chenille. The top floors are filled with morning sunshine, and the beds are good, even though they look like army issue. The one room with private facilities is not worth the extra outlay, unless you don't mind a portable corner unit with no air. You would be better off by saving the difference and using the clean hall toilets and showers instead.

English Spoken: Yes
Facilities & Services: None
Nearest Tourist Attractions: Campo Santa Tomà to Campo Santa Barnaba

AREA
Dorsoduro

TELEPHONE
(041) 522.58.17

FAX
None

TELEX
None

NUMBER OF ROOMS
11; w/BST, 1; w/o BST, 10

CREDIT CARDS
None

RATES
Single L40,000; double L60,000–70,000; triple L90,000; quad L120,000; hotel closed Nov 15–Jan 15; breakfast included

Locanda Montin ★
Fondamenta di Borgo, 1147

Exacting guests will probably want to look elsewhere. Others who thrive on nostalgia and funky charm will adore the Locanda Montin for its refreshing change from antiseptic anonymity. The hotel bears a faded look from years of attracting artists,

AREA
Dorsoduro

TELEPHONE
(041) 522.71.51

FAX
(041) 522.3307

TELEX
None

NUMBER OF ROOMS
7; w/BST, none; w/o BST, all

CREDIT CARDS
AMEX, DC, MC, V

RATES
Single L45,000; double L75,000; triple L90,000; quad L110,000; breakfast included

writers, and musicians on prolonged visits to Venice. As you walk up the stairs and along the corridors, you will see that the hotel is filled with a collection of original art from the fifties and sixties by artists who were regulars at Antica Locanda Montin, the popular, and now very trendy, restaurant below (see *Cheap Eats in Italy*, page 115). Now it is somewhat of a cult hotel, appealing to jolly groups of would-be bohemians who do not mind hall plumbing and thin walls.

It is becoming increasingly difficult to get a reservation. If you do succeed, you will be staying in a room that is filled to the brim with an assorted array of furnishings. If you are really lucky, you will get one of the two rooms with a flower-bedecked balcony that overlooks the canal. The hotel is conveniently situated just off Campo Santa Barnaba. It is not the easiest address to find, but once you reach the Fondamenta di Borgo, which runs off Calle Lunga Santa Barnaba, look for the black carriage lamp hanging over the front door with the name Locanda Montin marked on it.

English Spoken: Yes

Facilities & Services: None; 1 A.M. curfew

Nearest Tourist Attractions: Campo Santa Barnaba

Pensione Accademia ★★★
Fondamenta Bollani, 1058

AREA
Dorsoduro

TELEPHONE
(041) 523.78.46 or 521.01.88

FAX
(041) 523.91.52

TELEX
None

NUMBER OF ROOMS
27; w/BST, 21; w/o BST, 6

CREDIT CARDS
AMEX, DC, MC, V

The Pensione Accademia, occupying one of the most romantic settings in Venice just off the Grand Canal, offers charm and serene beauty at prices many can afford. It was built as a private mansion in the early 1900s, then used as the Russian consulate before World War II. It was also the fictional residence of Katherine Hepburn in *Summertime*. The stately villa is surrounded by lush gardens, which will give you the pleasant feeling of being a million miles away from the center of things, when actually you are only minutes away. On one side of the villa a graceful patio faces the canal, with tables and chairs placed among flowering plants. Along the other side is a garden with wisteria vines, fruit trees, and blooming rose bushes.

The inside is beautiful, with classic Murano chandeliers, Victorian and Venetian furnishings, and polished wooden floors. There is a cozy upstairs tearoom and a formally set breakfast room overlooking the rose garden. The adjoining bar has a wood-burning fireplace, which is lighted during the cool months. The nice rooms all vary, but have either canal or garden views. Number 8 is a delightful small room perfectly suited for one person. It has damask wallpaper and a pretty beamed ceiling with hand-painted accents. Number 7, a two-room suite facing the garden, is my choice for an extended stay. The rooms are large, with comfortable arm chairs, bureaus to settle into, and a bathroom with a glassed-in stall shower.

Reservations are essential at the Accademia, in some cases as much as a year in advance. The fiercely loyal clientele often reserve their favorite room or suite for the next year during this year's stay. It is the sort of place that once you check in, you never want to leave.

English Spoken: Yes

Facilities & Services: Some air-conditioned rooms, bar, direct-dial phones, TV & video in lounge

Nearest Tourist Attractions: Accademia Gallery, Guggenheim Collection, Accademia vaporetto stop nearby

Pensione Seguso ★★
Zattere al Gesuati, 779

The old-fashioned, elegantly upper-crust Seguso exudes an air of European tranquility that is rarely found anywhere today. The pensione serves breakfast, lunch, and dinner (and will even make picnics) to guests who enjoy gracious surroundings filled with antiques and family mementos, all for a price that a room alone costs in most Venetian hotels. While not for the traveler who likes marble, wall-to-wall carpeting, and uniformed porters, the Seguso is the ideal answer for the hopelessly romantic person who

RATES
Single L65,000–105,000; double L110,000–170,000; triple L205,000; breakfast L12,000 extra

AREA
Dorsoduro

TELEPHONE
(041) 522.23.40 or 528.68.58

FAX
(041) 522.2340

TELEX
None

NUMBER OF ROOMS
37; w/BST, 15; w/o BST, 22

CREDIT CARDS
AMEX, MC, V

RATES
Single L110,000–138,000;
double L85,000–210,000;
triple L250,000–300,000;
children 1–12 for 20% less;
room and breakfast in off
seasons only, otherwise half-
board required; breakfast
included; extra meal L35,000

yearns for the leisurely lifestyle that speaks of a bygone era.

In front there is a delightful terrace with tables set under colorful umbrellas. Breakfast and afternoon tea are served here while guests look out across the Giudecca Canal, which separates the main part of Venice from Giudecca Island. The homey rooms are decorated with tasteful simplicity. Some have ornate ceilings, others brass beds. Several overlook the terrace, and the prime ones overlook the canal, but these are bathless. However, these chambers all have sinks and share hall facilities with only one other room. The pensione has been in the Seguso family for over 70 years, and most of the staff have been with them for all of their working lives. Everyone is treated like family, and you will be too, making you feel, as most of the guests do, that this is a home away from home in Venice.

English Spoken: Yes
Facilities & Services: Lift, restaurant
Nearest Tourist Attractions: Accademia Gallery

SAN MARCO

Albergo San Zulian ★★
Calle San Zulian, 534

AREA
San Marco
TELEPHONE
(041) 522.58.72
FAX
(041) 523.22.65
TELEX
None
NUMBER OF ROOMS
18; all w/BST
CREDIT CARDS
AMEX, DC, MC, V
RATES
Single L120,000; double
L160,000; triple L190,000;
breakfast included and served in
rooms; lower off-season rates

From a Cheap Sleeper's viewpoint, the Albergo San Zulian offers sound comfort at rates that will not deplete a budget. The renovations at this hotel have put it well on the way to a top slot in the ranks of the better two-star hotels near St. Mark's Square. A nice balance has been struck between new and old, harmonized by fabrics and furnishings that recall Italy's artistic heritage and at the same time offer a splash of contemporary sophistication. The back stairs from a small ground-floor reception area done in white with black accents lead to rooms opening off the all-white corridors. The bedrooms are intelligently fitted with muted wall coverings, good closet space, and luggage racks, and some have pretty views over red tile roofs. Honeymooners will want to request Room No. 304, with its beautiful wooden beamed ceiling, mint-green Venetian-style furniture, and private terrace. Another special room is No. 104, a large double with Oriental throw rugs and a sofa with two chairs. This quiet, well-managed hotel is a good command post for walking to the Rialto Bridge area or to St. Mark's Square with all its fancy shops and sidewalk *caffès*. There is also a choice of good restaurants within a short stroll (see *Cheap Eats in Italy*).

English Spoken: Yes

Facilities & Services: Air-conditioning, direct-dial phones, hair dryers, mini-bars, private room safes, TVs

Nearest Tourist Attractions: Rialto Bridge, St. Mark's Square

Hotel Ala ★★★
Campo Santa Maria dei Giglio, 2494

For those wanting to be in the historic center of Venice, only minutes by foot from St. Mark's Square, the Hotel Ala is one answer. It is a neighbor of the famous Gritti Palace Hotel where rooms start at around $350 per night, so you know you are in an exclusive neighborhood. If romance is on the agenda during your stay here, plan to arrive at the hotel's private dock via gondola or water taxi.

While the hotel cannot be termed elegant, it does have a pleasing air about it. A large lounge and the breakfast room are hung with local artwork. These rooms also display Murano glass chandeliers, a mixture of old and new furniture, and an interesting collection of firearms. The rooms are inviting for long stays, because they have enough room for you and a few bags. Number 304, with Venetian painted furniture, beams, and red carpeting, looks out over the square below. The exceptional modern bathroom has mirrored and lighted glass over the sink, heated towel racks, and a combination tub and shower. The hotel operates the Ristorante da' Raffaele and offers discounts to guests who eat there. The setting alongside a canal is picture perfect and the food delicious, but hardly a Cheap Eat. However, with the

AREA
San Marco

TELEPHONE
(041) 520.53.33

FAX
(041) 520.36.90

TELEX
410275

NUMBER OF ROOMS
85; all w/BST

CREDIT CARDS
AMEX, DC, MC, V

RATES
Single L150,000; double L220,000: triple L260,000; 25% lower rates in off seasons; breakfast included

discount and careful planning, it would be a Big Splurge worth having.

English Spoken: Yes

Facilities & Services: Air-conditioning, bar, direct-dial phones, hair dryers, lift, mini-bars, some private safes, TVs

Nearest Tourist Attractions: St. Mark's Square, Grand Canal

Hotel do Pozzi ★★★
Via XXII Marzo, 2373

AREA
San Marco

TELEPHONE
(041) 520.78.55

FAX
(041) 522.9413

TELEX
420042 DPOZZI

NUMBER OF ROOMS
35; all w/BST

CREDIT CARDS
AMEX, DC, MC, V

RATES
Single L100,000–150,000; double L150,000–215,000; triple L200,000–250,000; quad L240,000–325,000; lower prices reflect off-season rates; breakfast included for L14,000 per person

For a moderately priced pick near St. Mark's Square, the do Pozzi is a good choice. The location is very quiet, yet central to the best shopping and most tourist must-do's in Venice. The coordinated modern-style bedrooms are not blessed with decorating overkill, but they are fully equipped with all the extras and have compact bathrooms. The best rooms are definitely the 12 that overlook the garden.

The hotel is part of a group that owns the Pensione Accademia (see page 136), the Hotel Ala (see page 139), and the canal-side Ristorante da' Raffaele. The restaurant offers a special half-board, two-course meal with dessert at 35,000 lire, or a 10 percent discount on à la carte choices to guests of these three hotels. This is a wonderfully romantic restaurant, especially at night if you sit outside on the terrace with someone you love and watch the serenading gondoliers float by in the moonlight.

English Spoken: Yes

Facilities & Services: Air-conditioning, bar, direct-dial phones, some hair dryers, laundry service, lift, mini-bars, room service for breakfast, TVs

Nearest Tourist Attractions: Shopping, St. Mark's Square

Hotel Flora ★★★
Calle Larga 22 Marzo, 2283A

AREA
San Marco

TELEPHONE
(041) 520.58.44

The Hotel Flora is a small Venetian hotel with the special ingredients of old-fashioned warmth and hospitality in evidence from the minute you arrive until you reluctantly leave. For many of its devotees, it is the perfect example of a romantic hotel to which many others are compared, but don't quite measure up. The hotel, which is owned and operated by Alex Romanelli and his son Roger, is done with beautiful taste and quality throughout. The entry is off Calle Larga XX Marzo, down a narrow lane where you can see the lovely garden through the glass doors as you arrive. This garden oasis in the middle of Venice is dominated by an old well and several pieces of statuary, and bordered by twisting vines and beds of hydrangeas, pansies, and camellia bushes. Breakfast and afternoon drinks are served here in the warm weather, and several of the rooms open onto it. During the cooler months, breakfast is served inside on English floral-print china, laid out on pink-covered round tables in a wood-paneled dining room with a walnut breakfront along one wall, accented by pieces of family silver and china. A beautiful hand-painted stairway leads to the bedrooms. The faux-finished furniture and damask-covered walls help to create an old-world feel. Some of the rooms are *very* small for one person, let alone two, so be sure to specify your size requirements when reserving and remember that the best rooms overlook the gardens. Prices are high for a basic Cheap Sleep, but if you choose this hotel for a Big Splurge, you will not be sorry.

English Spoken: Yes

Facilities & Services: Air-conditioning (L16,000 per day), bar, direct-dial phones, some hair dryers, lift for 3 floors, room service for breakfast

Nearest Tourist Attractions: St. Mark's Square, premier shopping

FAX
(041) 522.8217

TELEX
41001 FLORA I

NUMBER OF ROOMS
44; all w/BST

CREDIT CARDS
AMEX, DC, MC, V

RATES
Single L165,000; double L150,000–230,000; breakfast included; lower off-season rates; hotel is generally closed in Jan, and sometimes for remodeling in Nov and Dec; call to check as time varies

Hotel Gallini ★★
Calle de la Verona, 3673

Adriano Ceciliati and his brother have owned and personally managed the Gallini since 1950. Their friendly and hospitable approach to the hotel business has earned them an impressive roster of repeat visitors, many of whom consider this their Venetian home. Every year the hotel closes from November through February. How many hotels in the United States

AREA
San Marco

TELEPHONE
(041) 520.45.15

FAX
(041) 520.9103

TELEX
None

NUMBER OF ROOMS
50; w/BST, 43; w/o BST, 7
CREDIT CARDS
MC, V
RATES
Single L75,000–100,000;
double L100,000–140,000;
suite L170,000–210,000;
breakfast included; discounts
for guests not using a travel
agent for reservations; hotel
closed Nov–Mar 1

could do this and still stay in business? Not many, that is true. During this time they paint and do repairs and remodeling projects, so that when the hotel opens in March, everything is in perfect working order without any shabby edges. The basic bedrooms do not sizzle with personality, nor do they sport fine antiques or expensive fabrics. They are large enough to be comfortable, however, and spotless house-keeping standards are evident in every one. Those on the third floor are the best. The platinum location puts guests within easy walking distance of St. Mark's Square, La Fenice (the opera house), and the Rialto Bridge. The closest vaporetto stop is just a few minutes away on the Grand Canal.

English Spoken: Yes

Facilities & Services: Air-conditioned suites, direct-dial phones, TV in suites

Nearest Tourist Attractions: St. Mark's Square, La Fenice, Rialto Bridge

Hotel Kette ★★★
Piscine San Moisé, 2053

AREA
San Marco
TELEPHONE
(041) 520.77.66 or 522.27.30
FAX
(041) 522.89.64
TELEX
420653 KETTEV
NUMBER OF ROOMS
69; all w/BST
CREDIT CARDS
AMEX, DC, MC, V
RATES
Single L165,000; double
L220,000; triple L286,000;
quad L424,000; breakfast
included; lower winter rates

The Hotel Kette has it all. The prices may be high for some, but for those who want luxury for less, most will agree that its location between La Fenice and St. Mark's Square, its intimate atmosphere, and its friendly and efficient service make this choice worth the extra cost. By Venetian standards, the mid-18th-century building is "modern," but it has been renovated to a high standard while keeping the elegance and spirit of the original structure intact. The approach can be on foot through an intricate maze of winding streets, or via water at the private landing stage for gondolas just outside the hotel.

The lobby and public rooms are comfortably done, with soft sofas and chairs that invite you to spend long stays thumbing through one of the international magazines or daily papers provided for guests. The breakfast room is more contemporary than the rest of the hotel, with half-barrel chairs upholstered in velvet set around cloth-covered tables. The rooms vary in size and decor, but each has individual charm and a great deal of appeal. They are decorated with a nice combination of reproductions and newer pieces that blend together very well. Number 212, overlooking a little arbor-covered garden, gets my vote as an inviting choice for someone staying alone. For couples, No. 143 is a large double bedroom with a love seat, Oriental bedside rugs, a nice dressing table with mirrors, and a bath with the accessories we all want. Some of the rooms along the back look onto opposing walls. While they have all the facilities and nice furnishings of the other rooms in the hotel, they can be dark and gloomy, especially on short winter days.

English Spoken: Yes

Facilities & Services: Air-conditioning, direct-dial phones, hair dryers, lift, mini-bars, private room safes, TVs

Nearest Tourist Attractions: St. Mark's Square, Grand Canal

Hotel Locanda Fiorita ★
Campiello Nuovo, 3457

For my battered Cheap Sleeping buck, the Locanda Fiorita is without question one of the best one-star values in all of Venice. The ten-room hotel is off Campo S. Stefano on Campiello Nuovo, an inconspicuous square in the premier San Marco district. Once found, it promises to be a topic of conversation for those Cheap Sleepers who are looking for an affordable hotel that is smart, clean, and exceptionally nice. The entrance is upstairs, through a contemporary reception area with a beamed ceiling and a collection of Venetian Carnevale masks displayed on gray walls. Breakfast is served here around four tables with cane-seated bentwood chairs.

The thoughtfully redone rooms and baths are really amazing for a one-star, and for many two-stars for that matter. Each of the white-walled rooms has a beige carpet or tiled floors and a nice framed black and white print of Venice. There is also a small desk and a wardrobe big enough to hold more than the contents of a carry-on bag. The baths have stall

AREA
San Marco

TELEPHONE
(041) 523.47.54 or 522.80.43

FAX
None

TELEX
None

NUMBER OF ROOMS
10; w/BST, 7; w/o BST, 3

CREDIT CARDS
AMEX, MC, V

RATES
Single L50,000–85,000; double L80,000–115,000; extra person in room L35,000; breakfast included but can be deducted in off seasons; hotel closed Jan 10–25

showers and lighted mirrors over the sinks so you can see what you are doing while dressing for the day. Two of my favorite rooms are No. 1, a large double that opens onto a courtyard, and No. 9, another double with two view windows onto the street.

As you can imagine, word travels like wildfire about a find such as this one, so please get your reservation in just as soon as you know your arrival date in Venice.

English Spoken: Yes

Facilities & Services: Direct-dial phones

Nearest Tourist Attractions: St. Mark's Square, Campo S. Stefano

Hotel Noemi ★
Calle dei Fabbri, 909

AREA
San Marco

TELEPHONE
(041) 523.8144

FAX
(041) 522.52.38

TELEX
None

NUMBER OF ROOMS
15; w/BST, none; w/o BST, all

CREDIT CARDS
AMEX, DC, MC, V

RATES
Single L42,000; double L60,000; triple L83,000; breakfast L10,000 extra

The Noemi has many regulars who appreciate its location close to all the action and its has-been ambience. Those seeking more comfort and style should shop elsewhere. The mood here is old-fashioned, and so are the rates. The decor, if you can call it that, is rather mixed. Funny, red, low "leather-ette" seats gracing the small lobby contrast with the magnificent Murano glass banister along the stairs that lead to the 15 bathless chambers above. If you stay here you can expect some hall noise and plumbing gurgles from the sink in each room. The walls are decidedly thin, and you can only hope that your neighbors do not snore or play loud music. Some of the bedrooms could stand a fresh coat of paint, and the family antiques that are scattered about could use a little more attention from housekeeping. But—the prices of these rooms are impossible to top, and besides, who comes to Venice to linger indoors?

English Spoken: Yes

Facilities & Services: None

Nearest Tourist Attractions: St. Mark's Square

Hotel Riva ★
Ponte dell'Angelo, 5310

AREA
San Marco

I think of the Hotel Riva as the ideal place for a honeymoon couple on a budget, so long as space is not a top priority. What could be more wonderful than a stay in a revamped one-star hotel, perfectly positioned on a picturesque canal crisscrossed with bridges and filled with singing gondoliers plying their boats by the window? If romance was not part of your vacation plans before your arrival, it will be now.

Steep stairs lead from the attractive canal-side lobby and breakfast area to petite rooms that adopt a spare, yet functional approach to decorating. The furniture is mostly rustic, and the towels are *very* Italian, that is, thin and not too absorbent. Number 8, with a private bath, sleeps three and offers views of the San Marco church and the Canal dei Sospri below. The lilliputian singles have a twin bed squeezed into a room with no closet at all, only a coatrack, and barely enough space left over in which to change your mind. These are definitely to be avoided. However, if you ask for one of the largest rooms, you will be able to move around, and your room will have a view you will never forget.

English Spoken: Yes

Facilities & Services: Direct-dial phones planned

Nearest Tourist Attractions: St. Mark's Square

TELEPHONE
(041) 522.70.34

FAX
None

TELEX
None

NUMBER OF ROOMS
12; w/BST, 10; w/o BST, 2

CREDIT CARDS
None

RATES
Single L70,000; double L70,000–100,000; triple L130,000; breakfast included; closed in Dec

Hotel S. Giorgio ★★
Calle della Mandola, 3718

Humane prices and a golden location between the Rialto and St. Mark's puts guests here in shopping and sightseeing heaven. The combined sitting and breakfast room with faux-finished beige walls is highlighted by mirrors trimmed in soft blue and by Murano glass wall lights. Sofas in red velvet complement the blue chairs placed around circular dining tables. A glass display case shows off a large collection of crystal.

Once you pass through the sterile hospital-like hallways, the rooms are nice, if a bit overdone. All are different, but they do have curtains, carpets, and bedspreads that blend, and hand-painted furniture that puts the O on ornate. Number 14 is a flossy double with a pink velvet headboard and fringed bedside lamps. The bathroom is fine until you want

AREA
San Marco

TELEPHONE
(041) 523.58.35

FAX
(041) 522.8072

TELEX
None

NUMBER OF ROOMS
16; all w/BST

CREDIT CARDS
None

RATES
Single L100,000; double L140,000; triple L180,000; breakfast included

to take a shower or use the bidet; these two items are combined in one of the strangest pieces of plumbing equipment I have ever seen. Other choices are No. 11 with a double bed, a pull-down desk, and a large wardrobe closet; and No. 23, a twin done in dark woods and lighted by a crystal chandelier. Lower off-season rates add to the appeal of this hotel.

English Spoken: Yes

Facilities & Services: Air-conditioning available for 10% of room rate, direct-dial phones, mini-bars, TVs

Nearest Tourist Attractions: St. Mark's Square, Rialto Bridge

Hotel San Stefano ★★★
Campo S. Stefano, 2957

AREA
San Marco

TELEPHONE
(041) 520.01.66

FAX
(041) 522.4460

TELEX
None

NUMBER OF ROOMS
11; all w/BST

CREDIT CARDS
MC, V

RATES
Single L90,000–140,000; double L155,000–190,000; triple L195,000–245,000; breakfast included

One of the best quality-to-price ratios in this section of Venice is the Hotel San Stefano. It is located right on the active and colorful Campo Santa Stefano, which boasts a pretty church, locals sunning themselves on benches, and the *gelateria* Paolin, which scoops up some of the best ice cream in Venice (see *Cheap Eats in Italy*, page 124). The hotel is intimate and charming, with views onto the square from many of the rooms. A tiny garden patio provides a place for warm-weather breakfasts or a calm oasis for postcard writing.

The comfortable and compact rooms are thoughtfully done and attractively decorated with hand-painted furniture, subdued fabrics including watered silk, and crystal lights. If you are a light sleeper, ask for a room away from the square, as it gets noisy sometimes at night, especially in the summer. During the off seasons, good discounts are offered and chances are you will not need the air-conditioner, so you will save even more money.

English Spoken: Yes

Facilities & Services: Air-conditioning L10,000–15,000, depending on size of room; direct-dial phones; hair dryers; lift; TVs

Nearest Tourist Attractions: St. Mark's Square, Accademia Gallery, Grand Canal

Locanda Casa Petrarca ★
Calle degli Schiavine, 4386

You probably would never find the Locanda Casa Petrarca if someone did not tip you off about it ahead of time. When you book your room, Nellie, the hospitable English-speaking owner, will give you specific directions on how to get to her seven-room hideaway tucked at the end of Calle degli Schiavine. As you approach it, look for the flower boxes in the archway windows by the main entrance. The rooms redefine *tiny*, but they are clean and cheerful, with tiled floors, bedside rugs, and the type of modern furniture you would put in a child's room. There is a small reception area done in wicker and green plants, but no breakfast room, so it will be served to you in your room, which could add a romantic touch to your stay, depending on your roommate.

English Spoken: Yes

Facilities & Services: None

Nearest Tourist Attractions: St. Mark's Square, Rialto Bridge

AREA
San Marco

TELEPHONE
(041) 520.04.30

FAX
None

TELEX
None

NUMBER OF ROOMS
7; w/BST, 4; w/o BST, 3

CREDIT CARDS
None; cash only

RATES
Single L45,000; double L50,000–80,000; extra person 35% of room rate; showers L3,000 including towel but no soap; breakfast L8,500 extra

SAN POLO

Hotel Carpaccio ★★★
Rio Pisani Barbarigo, off Rio Terra dei Nomboli, San Tomà 2765

Originally, guests approached this building floating down the Grand Canal via gondola, not by foot, which is now the only access. Located in the heart of the oldest part of Venice with its maze of winding streets, the Carpaccio is accessible only to the determined visitor armed with a detailed street map. The hotel is definitely worth the search, if only for its million-dollar views of the Grand Canal. Amazingly enough, rooms without a view cost the same as rooms with them. So is there any choice? I don't think so.

Unfortunately, the style of the bedrooms does not live up to the architecture of the building, or to the pretty salon with polished marble floors and a commanding view through an arched window right onto the Grand Canal. Done in landlord green and

AREA
San Polo

TELEPHONE
(041) 523.59.46

FAX
(041) 524.21.34

TELEX
None

NUMBER OF ROOMS
20; w/BST, 17; w/o BST, 3

CREDIT CARDS
MC, V

RATES
Single L85,000–140,000; double L140,000–205,000; extra bed L45,000–60,000; breakfast included; hotel closed Nov–Feb.

fifties' furniture, the rooms can charitably be described as dated and in some instances, downright ugly. However, this is *not* a reason to go elsewhere. The rooms are clean, the beds are good, space is abundant, and those picture-postcard views more than make up for the questionable taste.

Note: The hotel is closed from November 1 through February.

English Spoken: Yes

Facilities & Services: Bar, direct-dial phones

Nearest Tourist Attractions: Campo San Tomà, Grand Canal

Hotel da Pino ★
Crosera S. Pantalon, 3941–2

AREA
San Polo

TELEPHONE
(041) 522.36.46

FAX
None

TELEX
None

NUMBER OF ROOMS
16; w/BST, 1; w/o BST, 15

CREDIT CARDS
None

RATES
Single L35,000; double L48,000; triple L26,000 per person; breakfast L6,000 extra

Simplicity prevails in the down-to-earth bedrooms and public areas of da Pino. The 16 clean-as-a-whistle chambers are located on the main shopping street, which cuts through San Polo near the university section in Venice. For soaking up the atmosphere of Venetian life, you cannot beat this area. There are lots of good restaurants (see *Cheap Eats in Italy*), bars, *caffès*, shops, and piazzas with outdoor markets. Not too far away is the only floating market in Venice, along the Rio di San Barnaba. For the moment, the hotel is open to guests in July and August, from December 15 until January 1, and at Easter. During the rest of the year, it is filled with students who are studying at the university. However, by the end of 1993, the owner and his mother plan to have some rooms available year round.

English Spoken: Yes

Facilities & Services: None

Nearest Tourist Attractions: Close to the Grand Canal and 2 vaporetto stops (San Tomà and Ca' Rezzonico)

Locanda Sturion ★★
Calle del Sturion, 679

AREA
San Polo

If you dream of a room with a Grand Canal view, but have nightmares when thinking of the astronomical prices most hotels charge, fret no more and check into the Locanda Sturion. Just a year ago it was a dingy spot frequented by down-and-outers squeezing their last few lire to the max. Now, thanks to a complete rehabilitation, it is a spiffy two-star hotel that can be recommended without reservation. The surroundings are well designed and quiet. The best rooms are the two large ones overlooking the Grand Canal. Though not luxurious, the rooms have features many three-star hotels wish they had. The bathrooms are beautifully tiled in shades of pink and mauve. The lighted mirrors over the sinks are bordered with an artistic tile frame, and the heated towel racks keep the cotton towels ready for the next shower. Your breakfast will be served in a pretty dining room with a canal view. You will no doubt want to linger here over a second cup of coffee or roll while scribbling a few postcards to friends back home, suggesting you may never return from Venice.

Warning: For most, the four flights of stairs to the reception area and hotel proper will be a piece of cake, but for committed couch potatoes, they might pose a problem.

English Spoken: Yes

Facilities & Services: Air-conditioning, bar, direct-dial phones, hair dryers, mini-bars, private room safes, TVs

Nearest Tourist Attractions: Rialto Bridge

TELEPHONE
(041) 523.62.43

FAX
(041) 522.8370

TELEX
None

NUMBER OF ROOMS
11; all w/BST

CREDIT CARDS
MC, V

RATES
Single L90,000; double L125,000; triple L160,000; quad L196,000; breakfast included; lower off-season rates

SANTA CROCE

Albergo Casa Peron ★
Calle Vinati, 84–85

This heaven-sent retreat for Cheap Sleepers is in a calm neighborhood midway between Piazzale Roma and the Grand Canal. Giannco Scarpa and his wife take great pride in their hotel, and it shows from the minute you step into the lobby and reach your tidy bedroom until you sit on the peaceful upstairs terrace filled with fragrant jasmine, roses, vines, and flowering plants. The Scarpas live in their hotel and are dedicated to every detail, from monitoring the housekeeping staff to discouraging room picnics and

AREA
Santa Croce

TELEPHONE
(041) 528.60.38

FAX
None

TELEX
None

NUMBER OF ROOMS
11+6 student; w/BST, none, but all have shower; w/o BST, 11 without toilet

loud guests. There are two parts to the hotel. If I were a student again, I would definitely check into the student annex, where the rooms are immaculate but not inspirational. The havens in the other part are just as fastidiously maintained. Some have balconies with rooftop views. All are sunny and bright, with bare-bones furniture displaying not a nick or a scratch. A few have private bathrooms, yet all have private showers. While the prices are not in the champion price-slasher category, they are extremely competitive and offer some of the best value for the money.

English Spoken: Yes

Facilities & Services: None

Nearest Tourist Attractions: Interesting neighborhood; 15 minutes to vaporetto stop on Grand Canal

CREDIT CARDS
None; cash only

RATES
Single L48,000–58,000; double L78,000–95,000; triple L110,000–125,000; quad L150,000; breakfast included but may be deducted (L7,000) on request

Hotel Falier ★★
Salizzada San Pantalon, 130

AREA
Santa Croce

TELEPHONE
(041) 522.88.82 or 521.00.05

FAX
(041) 520.6554

TELEX
None

NUMBER OF ROOMS
19; all w/BST

CREDIT CARDS
MC, V

RATES
Single L90,000; double L125,000; breakfast included; lower off-season rates

Completely restyled from top to bottom in 1992, the Hotel Falier is on my short list of favorite two-star hotels in Venice. It is well located and close to Piazzale Roma (where you can park your car if you have one while visiting Venice) and the train station. The area is not touristy, but it is lined with good neighborhood restaurants and some interesting shops that are fun to stroll by and to browse through. The stylish open lobby with its columns, French furniture, and potted palms faces the street and the canal that runs along the front. At the back of the lobby is a corner breakfast area with nice banquette seating where you can watch the equivalent of "Good Morning America" on television while drinking strong coffee and eating rolls and jam. Each room, though small, reflects excellent taste. I like their uniformity, lacy window curtains, flowered bedspreads, built-in furniture, luggage racks, and modern bathrooms with good shelf space. The hotel is part of the Family Hotel and Restaurant Association in Italy, which always means a friendly and pleasant stay for guests.

English Spoken: Yes

Facilities & Services: Direct-dial phones, hair dryers, lift

Nearest Tourist Attractions: Close to train station and parking, Campo S. Rocco, Frari Church

LIDO ISLAND

Lido Island is about 20 minutes from St. Mark's Square by water taxi. Here you will find family pensiones that serve three meals a day and a place to park your car, avoiding the expense and anxiety of leaving it at one of the public parking garages at Piazzale Roma. Tourists come to Lido by the thousands during the warm months, drawn by the casino, the society life (greatly diminished, but still fun for some), and the long stretch of beach. Unless you are staying at a hotel that has beach cabanas, it will be difficult to find a clean spot even along the best sections of the beach, for you will be relegated to the public beaches at the northern and southern ends of the island where the water is not clean. But even if you do not go to the beach, you can still play tennis or golf, water ski, wind surf, ride horses, and try your luck at parasailing.

Hotel Atlanta Augustus ★★★
Via Lepanto, 15

The motto at the Hotel Atlanta Augustus is "Cleanliness and comfort." With this unbeatable combination, it is no wonder that it has such a loyal clientele. While there is nothing elegant or regal about the hotel, it does have a warm and friendly atmosphere, thanks to owner Ricardo Polacco, who makes every effort to see that his guests have enjoyable stays. The liberty-style villa has 31 modern bedrooms with no surprises. A few rooms with pretty canal views, security parking, and beach cabanas on the Lido beach are three appealing extras for many. A larger-than-average breakfast consisting of hard-cooked eggs, two types of bread, cheese, ham, and salami provides enough energy for the day until you return to the American bar, which features a nightly happy hour.

AREA
Lido

TELEPHONE
(041) 526.12.05 or 526.05.69

FAX
(041) 526.5604

TELEX
None

NUMBER OF ROOMS
31; all w/BST

CREDIT CARDS
MC, V

RATES
Single L110,000–150,000; double L160,000–206,000; triple L180,000–250,000; quad L200,000–300,000; breakfast included; lower rates for longer stays and in off seasons

Because there are no meals served other than breakfast, vouchers are given for the restaurant next door.

English Spoken: Yes

Facilities & Services: Some air-conditioning at 10% of room rate; bar; direct-dial phones; lift; free parking for stays of 3 days or longer, otherwise L10,000 per day; beach cabanas

Nearest Tourist Attractions: Lido

Hotel Belvedere ★★★
Piazza le Santa Maria Elisabetta, 4

AREA
Lido
TELEPHONE
(041) 526.0115 or 526.0164
FAX
(041) 526.1486
TELEX
None
NUMBER OF ROOMS
30; all w/BST
CREDIT CARDS
All
RATES
Single L149,000; double L198,000; triple L248,000; breakfast included; lower off-season rates; closed 1 week in Nov

The Belvedere has been owned and managed by the same family since it was built in 1857. It is well situated, overlooking the lagoon, and is only about ten minutes away from Venice by water bus or private motorboat. The rooms have been modernized and are enhanced by dedicated upkeep. Although they are dependable, their cookie-cutter style is bland and unimaginative. They are, however, spotless, and so are the bathrooms. The hotel is open 51 weeks of the year and has parking, two important features appreciated by many guests. The hotel also operates a good restaurant and a snack bar, but they are closed on Mondays and from November to April (see *Cheap Eats in Italy*, page 133). A final bonus is the lower off-season rates, which make this a smart Cheap Sleep stopover on expensive Lido Island.

English Spoken: Yes

Facilities & Services: Air-conditioning in 10 rooms, direct-dial phones, lift, free parking, restaurant and snack bar, TVs and radios

Nearest Tourist Attractions: Lido; 10 minutes by boat to Venice proper

Hotel Centrale & Byron ★★★
Via Bragadin, 30

AREA
Lido
TELEPHONE
(041) 526.00.52 or 526.02.91

The Centrale & Byron is a comfortable old hotel that has been well tended over the years. The garden setting is midway between the wharf, which is a ten-minute boat ride to St. Mark's Square, and the white-sand Lido beach. As you walk into the lobby, you will see that this hotel was something in its heyday. The formal dining room, with its soft yellow walls and white accents, faux marble pillars, and chandeliers, is a welcoming haven after a long day of foot-weary sightseeing in Venice. There is a fully stocked American bar and a garden with tables and chairs inviting lazy afternoon stays. The rooms, with coordinated colors, wooden floors, and modern furniture have all the comforts and plenty of storage. The baths are starting to show their age, but they are scrupulously clean. Nine more rooms have beach views and cost not one lira more than those that do not. The management and uniformed staff are warmly professional, and do everything they can to make your stay as pleasant as possible.

English Spoken: Yes

Facilities & Services: Air-conditioning L10,000 per day; bar; no central heat, only portable units; direct-dial phones; lift; mini-bars; private room safes; restaurant for 3 meals a day; TVs

Nearest Tourist Attractions: Lido

FAX
(041) 526.9241

TELEX
None

NUMBER OF ROOMS
36; all w/BST

CREDIT CARDS
AMEX, DC, MC, V

RATES
Single L100,000; double L160,000; triple L180,000; suite L220,000; closed Nov–Dec; breakfast included but can be deducted at L18,000 per person

Hotel Villa Pannonia ★★
Via Doge D. Michiel, 48

One of the best two-star hotels on Lido is the Villa Pannonia. There are several reasons for this. First of all, the owner and his family are always present at the hotel. Second, the clean and serviceable rooms have pretty garden views, compact bathrooms, and easy-care modern furniture. Finally, the restaurant, which offers full- or half-board and is open only to hotel guests, has a chef who will take the time to meet special diet requests. This family-style hotel has been going strong since 1905, catering to a core of regulars who spend their vacations here year after year. It has seen several renovation projects, yet it retains a degree of familiar provincialism that is pleasing. Beach cabanas with chairs cost 12,000 lire each and are an essential ingredient for a day on the Lido beach. If you do not rent a cabana, you are banished to an end of the beach that is not desirable. The hotel is closed from Christmas through January, and the restaurant

AREA
Lido

TELEPHONE
(041) 526.0162

FAX
(041) 526.5277

TELEX
None

NUMBER OF ROOMS
32; w/BST, 30; w/o BST, 2

CREDIT CARDS
AMEX, DC, MC, V

RATES
Single L58,000–89,000; double L124,000; triple L160,000; quad L180,000; adjoining rooms L220,000; hotel closed Christmas–January; half-board and room L85,000 per person; full-board and room L90,000 per person; breakfast included

serves lunch and dinner only from April until November 10. Cheap Sleepers will be happy to know that discounted rates are available in the off seasons—please ask for them.

English Spoken: Yes

Facilities & Services: Bar, direct-dial phones, free parking

Nearest Tourist Attractions: Lido

Villa Aurora ★★
Riviera S. Nicolo 11A

AREA	Lido
TELEPHONE	(041) 526.05,19
FAX	(041) 526.0519
TELEX	None
NUMBER OF ROOMS	18; w/BST, 15; w/o BST, 3
CREDIT CARDS	None
RATES	Single L23,000–45,000; double L40,000–90,000; extra person L25,000; hotel usually closed Jan 8–Carnevale; breakfast L5,000 extra

For the best budget bet on Lido, check into the Villa Aurora. Not only are the prices good, but they actually *go down* the longer you stay. Once you get by the tacky furniture in the plain rooms, you will realize that they are well suited to the lifestyle of the frugal. Several have direct views of the lagoon in front and of a canal along the side. As for noise, there is some. It comes from the busy thoroughfare that runs by the hotel and from guests talking too loudly in the halls. The hotel operates a pizzeria next door, which offers a low 20,000-lire set menu in addition to all the pizza favorites. Finally, you can not beat the location, close to the landing stages with ferries to take you to neighboring islands and across to Venice itself.

English Spoken: No, not always

Facilities & Services: Lift

Nearest Tourist Attractions: Lido

OTHER OPTIONS

CAMPING

Some of the Cheapest Sleeps in Venice are in a tent under the stars. The campgrounds have the disadvantage of being at least 30 minutes to one hour away from tourist interests in Venice, and they require long commutes by bus followed by vaporetto rides. In some locations, there is the further disadvantage of having to catch the last bus by 10 P.M., then walking from the bus stop to the campground in the dark. However, for nature lovers and diehard Cheap Sleepers, the price is as cheap as you will get.

Camping Fusina
Via Moranzani

Area: Fusina
Telephone: (041) 547.00.55
Credit Cards: MC, V
English: Yes
Open: Year around
Rates: L7,000 per person, plus: caravan L18,000 per day; tent L18,000 per day; camper L12,500 per day

This campground is 20 minutes by boat to Venice or 1 1/2 hours by bus. There is a store, a restaurant, and a bar, and the showers are free. Space for 10,000 people.

Ca' Pasquall
Via Fausta, 33

Area: Outside of Venice
Telephone: (041) 96.61.10
Credit Cards: AMEX
English: Yes
Open: May 10–Sept 17
Rates: L6,500 per person, children 1–5 L5,000, plus: tent L19,500; caravan L19,500

The campgrounds have 2,000 places, a store, a restaurant, and a swimming pool. There is a three-day minimum stay.

Marina de Venezia
Punta Sabbioni, Via Montello, 6

A pretty setting. The campground has a restaurant, a bar, and a market.

Area: Outside of Venice
Telephone: (041) 966.146
Credit Cards: None; cash only
English: Yes
Open: Year around
Rates: Camping L8,000 per person, children 1–6 L6,000, plus: tent, car, or caravan L22,000; bungalow for 4 L95,000, for 7 L135,000 (no linens)

APARTMENT RENTALS
International Services (see Rome, page 110)

STUDENT ACCOMMODATIONS
In the summer and during Christmas and Easter vacation, accommodations to please most hard-core Cheap Sleeper budgets can be found in dormitories run by various schools and religious organizations. These are Spartan at best. Some have strict rules and regulations, most have curfews, some have daytime lockouts, and a few serve low-cost meals.

Domus Cavanis
Rio Terra Foscarini, 899

Area: Dorsoduro
Telephone: (041) 522.28.26 or 522.85.05
Credit Cards: None; cash only
English: Limited
Open: June–Sept
Rates: L50,000–55,000 per person, breakfast included

Catholic-run, with separate quarters for men and women. Not the cheapest, but an excellent central location in Venice. Dinner is served.

Domus Civica
Calle Campazzo, 3082

Open only to women. Near the train station. Double rooms with hot and cold running water and free showers. Office open 7:30 A.M.–11:30 A.M. Curfew at 11:30 P.M.

Area: San Polo
Telephone: (041) 522.71.39
Credit Cards: None; cash only
English: Yes
Open: June 1–Oct 15
Rates: L22,000 per person

Foresteria Valdese
Calle Lunga S. Maria Formosa, 5170

Area: Castello
Telephone: (041) 528.67.97

Credit Cards: None; cash only
English: Yes
Open: All year
Rates: L27,000 per person in dorm room, breakfast included

Venice's largest Protestant church runs this student hostel. Registration is from 9:30 A.M.–1 P.M. and 6–8 P.M. There are two nice double rooms, but reservations are required months in advance for these.

Istituto Cannosiano
Fondamenta del Ponte Piccolo, 428

   Area: Giudecca Island
   Telephone: (041) 522.21.57
   Credit Cards: None; cash only
   English: Limited
   Open: Year around
   Rates: L15,000 per person in dorm rooms

Run by nuns and open only to women. Not the friendliest environment. Lockout from rooms: 8:30 A.M.–4 P.M.; registration: 9 A.M.–noon and 4–6 P.M.

Istituto Ciliota
Calle delle Muneghe, 2976

   Area: San Marco
   Telephone: (041) 520.48.88
   Credit Cards: None; cash only
   English: Yes
   Open: June 7–September 25
   Rates: Single L40,000; double L65,000; includes breakfast

Run by nuns and friendly. Curfew at 11 P.M.

Istituto S. Giuseppi
Calle Cassellaria, 5420

   Area: Castello
   Telephone: (041) 522.53.52
   Credit Cards: None; cash only
   English: Yes
   Open: All year except for Christmas and Easter
   Rates: L25,000 per person

Accommodations are in dorm-style rooms. The central location has a garden. They prefer families. Guests must reserve one month in advance and send a deposit.

Ostello Venezia
Fondamenta di Zitelle, 86

Area: Giudecca Island
Telephone: (041) 523.82.11
Credit Cards: None; cash only
English: Yes
Open: Year around to members of IYHF only
Rates: L15,000 per person in dorm rooms with 4–20 persons

Open only to holders of the IYHF (International Youth Hostel Federation) card, which must be presented along with a passport at registration. Draconian rules: you must pay for sheets and blankets; there is no smoking; you must vacate your room each day from 9 A.M.–6 P.M.; you cannot check out before 7:30 A.M.; you can only check in from 6–11:00 P.M. Dinner is served from 6–9 P.M. Lockout is at 11 P.M.; lights are turned off at 11:30 P.M.

Suore Mantellate
Calle Buccari, 10

Area: S. Elena
Telephone: (041) 522.08.29
Credit Cards: None; cash only
English: Limited
Open: Sept–July, closed Aug
Rates: Single L33,000; double L65,400; breakfast included

A long walk from St. Mark's Square. The rooms are large, and the nuns are hospitable.

SHOPPING: CHEAP CHIC

Throughout history, the Italians have known and appreciated good taste and fine quality. The rest of the world recognizes the "made in Italy" label as often the best available. The high quality of Italian life is evident everywhere you look, from good food and wine to beautiful clothing, the latest in furniture designs, and unique handicrafts. In these days of standardization and mass production, Italian artisans are still creating original and beautiful objects. Italian ceramics, embroidery and lace, gold and silver jewelry, glassware, and paper and leather goods have established Italy as the leader in the world market.

As everyone knows, Italy is also one of the world's leading centers for fashion, and many believe that the Italians are some of the best-dressed people in Europe, if not the world. They dress with such style, and look with disdain at foreigners dressed in shorts and T-shirts and wearing a pair of sandals or the latest in athletic shoes, all in the name of "I am on a vacation and *will* be comfortable at all costs."

If you are a born shopper, you will not be able to spend all of your time eating, sleeping, and sightseeing. You will have to do some shopping just to maintain equilibrium (i.e., sanity). It is sad but true that the days of finding one bargain after another in Italy are *over*. The dollar buys about 30 to 40 percent less than it did just ten years ago. That, along with soaring inflation, has made shopping in Italy almost prohibitive. Do not give up hope; all is not completely lost, especially if you are armed with "Cheap Chic," and can follow some of the guidelines given. You will undoubtedly find some wonderful things to take home with you and enjoy for a lifetime.

The government regulates the duration of sales and the amount a store can discount. There are two sale periods allowed by law each year: from mid-January until the end of February, and all of July. This is a great time to buy, as prices are cut by as much as 50 percent on top-quality goods, not cheap items brought in especially for the sale. During nonsale times, look for shops with signs saying *sconti* ("discounts") or *vendita promozionale* ("promotional sale"). These are not government-sanctioned sales, and the discounts will be lower, but it is definitely worth a Cheap Chic shopper's look.

The following shops are by no means all there are. They are only suggestions to get you started on a great shopping adventure of your own. I wish you good luck and happy shopping.

CHEAP CHIC SHOPPING TIPS

1. When you see it, like it, want it, and the price suits your budget— buy it. Do not comparison shop or plan to think it over, because you probably won't have time, or, if you do, the item will be gone and you will never see it again.

2. Pack an empty soft folding suitcase in your luggage so you can bring your purchases home with you and not go to the expense of mailing and insuring. If the airline charges you an excess baggage fee (usually around $100), for the extra bag, it will still be cheaper than mailing.

3. Do some preliminary shopping research before you leave home. Make a list of sizes, and check prices in your local stores. That way, you will know a bargain when you see one and have some focus on your shopping. However, do not get stuck sticking to an exact list. Be flexible.

4. At flea markets, you can expect about a 10 to 20 percent discount as a result of bargaining. You will always get the best price if you can pay cash.

5. Never change money in a store. Always go to a bank for the best rate.

6. Bring a pocket calculator to avoid asking, "How much is that in dollars?"

7. Nothing is returnable. Buy with care.

8. Remember that the big sales are held from mid-January through February, and in July. The price reduction on top goods can be as much as 50 percent.

9. Keep a log of your purchases, along with the receipts to show what you paid and the equivalent in U.S. dollars. This will make it easier to fill out the customs forms.

10. Each person receives a $400 duty-free allowance. This applies *only* to items you carry home with you. Everyone in your group who is on the trip with you gets this allowance, so if you are over, apply your extra to any of your companions who are under the limit.

DETASSE (EXPORT TAX)

Most shopkeepers deny its existence, but it is there. Frankly, after going through all the hassle and red tape, you will probably wish you had never heard of it. It works this way: If you spend *over* 626,000 lire in one store, you are eligible. However, rather than go through all the paperwork, some stores will offer you a discount to forget the tax. Best advice: Take the *sconto* ("discount") and run!

SIZE CONVERSION CHART

WOMEN'S DRESSES, COATS, AND SKIRTS

American	3	5	7	9	11	12	13	14	15	16	18
Continental	36	38	38½	40	40½	42	42½	44	44	46	48

WOMEN'S BLOUSES AND SWEATERS

American	10	12	14	16	18	20
Continental	38	40	42	44	46	48

WOMEN'S HOSIERY

American	8	8½	9	9½	10	10½
Continental	1	2	3	4	5	6

WOMEN'S SHOES

American	5	6	7	8	9	10
Continental	36	37	38	39	40	41

CHILDREN'S CLOTHING

American	3	4	5	6	6X
Continental	98	104	110	116	122

CHILDREN'S SHOES

American	8	9	10	11	12	13	1	2	3
Continental	24	25	27	28	29	30	32	33	34

MEN'S SUITS

American	34	36	38	40	42	44	46	48
Continental	44	46	48	50	52	54	56	58

MEN'S SHIRTS

American	14½	15	15½	16	16½	17	17½	18
Continental	37	38	39	41	42	43	44	45

MEN'S SHOES

American	7	8	9	10	11	12	13
Continental	39½	41	42	43	44½	46	47

Note: Sizing is not standardized in Italy, and often you will find different fits in the same size. It is important to remember that many stores offer complimentary alterations (*alterazioni*).

SHOPPING IN FLORENCE

SHOPPING HOURS

Winter: Mon afternoon and Tue–Sat, 9 A.M.–1 P.M. and 3:30–7:30 P.M.; closed Mon morning

Summer: Afternoon hours 4–8 P.M.; closed Sat afternoon and all or part of Aug

Yearly: Food shops closed Wed afternoon

Florence has long been renowned for its wonderful shopping. The number of shops is large, but the city's small size puts almost everything within walking distance in a relatively short time. Florentine artists today maintain the same high level of originality and attention to detail as they did centuries ago. Many families have worked in the same shops for generations and thus take enormous pride in the workmanship that bears their name and upholds their reputation for quality.

The specialties of Florence are hand-embroidered linens, gold, ceramics, leather, handmade paper goods, and bookbinding. In Florence you will also find a sampling of Italy's best merchandise, from the traditional and antique to perfect reproductions and the avant-garde. In many shops, the prices are as high as the quality. So where does that leave the Cheap Chic shopper? First of all, remember that you are getting top quality for your money, so be prepared to spend just a little more and forget all about finding "a steal." Next, shop in the outdoor markets at San Lorenzo Central Market and the Straw Market, as well as the many small shops where you will be able to find imaginative items that fit into even the slimmest budgets.

After Dark Bookstore
Via del Moro, 86
TELEPHONE 29.42.03
HOURS Mon–Sat 10 A.M.–1:30 P.M. and 3–7 P.M.
CREDIT CARDS AMEX, DC, MC, V
TYPE Bookshop

An excellent selection of English-language books and popular American magazines such as *The New Yorker* and *People*. Also cards, gift wrap, postcards, and used books. Owner Norman Grant will let you trade in your guidebooks for other used ones he stocks. You can also bring in your used books and get credit toward anything in the store.

Angela Caputi
Borgo San Jacopo, 78/82
TELEPHONE 21.29.72

HOURS Mon 3:30–7:30 P.M., Tues–Sat 10 A.M.–1 P.M.

CREDIT CARDS AMEX, DC, MC, V

TYPE Jewelry and dresses

All of the jewelry is designed by Angela Caputi, and it is wonderful, but not for the conservative minded. A few doors down is the dress shop, which also features unusual designs. Don't miss these shops if you want something different and striking.

Balloon
Via del Proconsolo, 69

TELEPHONE 21.24.60

HOURS Mon 3:30–7:30 P.M., Tues–Sat 10 A.M.–1 P.M. and 3:30–7:30 P.M.

CREDIT CARDS MC, V

TYPE Current fashions

Balloon has shops in major Italian cities (see Rome, page 172). They specialize in a well-priced selection of clothes for people thirtysomething. Lots of things are made in China, so check carefully for quality.

Bijoux Casico
Via Por S. Maria, 1, or Via Tornabuoni, 32

TELEPHONE 294.378

HOURS Mon–Sat 9:30 A.M.–1 P.M. and 3:30–7:30 P.M.; closed Mon morning in winter, closed Sat afternoon June–Sept

CREDIT CARDS AMEX, DC, MC, V

TYPE Costume jewelry

Fabulous fake jewelry.

Biondetti
Piazza degli Aldobrandini, 11; near San Lorenzo Central Market

TELEPHONE 28.19.55

HOURS Mon 3:30–7:30 P.M., Tues–Sat 9 A.M.–1:00 P.M. and 3:30–7:30 P.M.

CREDIT CARDS MC, V

TYPE Notions

Even if you do not sew a stitch, you will be inspired by this intriguing shop selling ribbons, sew-ons, unusual buttons, trims, and every shade of thread imaginable. If you do sew, this is the place for you. There are ideas galore.

BM Bookshop
Via Borgo Ognissani, 4

TELEPHONE AND FAX 29.45.75

HOURS Winter: Mon 3:30–7:30 P.M., Tues–Sat 9:30 A.M.–1 P.M. and 3:30–7:30 P.M.; summer: 9:30 A.M.–1 P.M. and 3:30–7:30 daily

CREDIT CARDS AMEX, MC, V

TYPE Bookshop

An excellent selection of English-language books specializing in art, travel, paperback fiction, cooking, design, fashion. Also a good selection of videos. They will ship. Very friendly owners.

Cartoleria in Firenze
Via del Parione, 10

TELEPHONE 21.56.84

HOURS Mon–Sat 9 A.M.–8 P.M.

CREDIT CARDS AMEX, DC, MC, V

TYPE Paper goods

This shop specializes in Florentine and handmade decorative papers, desk accessories, Christmas cards, and stationery. They will ship.

Coin Department Store
Via dei Calzaiuoli, 56

HOURS Mon–Sat 9:30 A.M.–1 P.M. and 3:30–7:30 P.M.; closed Mon morning in winter

CREDIT CARDS AMEX, DC, MC, V

TYPE Dry goods

Italy's answer to J.C. Penney's. A good houseware selection in the basement.

Dino Bartolini
Via dei Servi, 30

TELEPHONE 21.18.95

HOURS Tues–Sat 9 A.M.–1 P.M. and 3:30–7:30 P.M.; closed Aug and all day Mon

CREDIT CARDS None

TYPE Kitchenware

Every kitchen item you have ever heard of and many you never have. Also a fine selection of china, pottery, crystal, silver, and plates for collectors.

English Bookstore and Paperback Exchange
Via Fiesolana, 3

TELEPHONE 24.78.154

HOURS Mon–Sat 9 A.M.–1 P.M. and 3:30–7:30 P.M.; closed Mon Nov–Feb, closed Aug

CREDIT CARDS AMEX, DC, MC, V

TYPE Bookshop

The unofficial community center for English-speaking tourists and residents in Florence. They have new and used books on art history, humanities, Italian studies, political science, travel, and popular fiction. They will trade their second-hand books for your second-hand books.

Eusebio
Via del Corso, 1–11

TELEPHONE 21.37.80

HOURS Mon–Sat 9 A.M.–1 P.M. and 3–8 P.M.; closed Mon morning in winter

CREDIT CARDS None

TYPE Shoe store

Discount shoes for men and women. The quality is uneven, so look carefully. At their sport shoe shop (Via del Corso, 39) there is a good selection, but the prices are not as low as for dress shoes.

Farmacia Münstermann
Piazza Goldoni, 2

TELEPHONE 21.06.60

HOURS Mon–Fri 9 A.M.–1 P.M. and 4–8 P.M.; closed Sat, Sun, 15 days after Christmas and 15 days in Aug

CREDIT CARDS MC, V

TYPE Pharmacy and cosmetics

Clarissa Petruzzi is carrying on the tradition of her parents in running this wonderful pharmacy and cosmetic shop. Here you can buy her handmade natural and homeopathic cosmetics, which have been carefully prepared and packaged in the old-fashioned manner. There is a fine stock of products for body and sun care, skin and hair, and fragrances for men and women. There is a catalog available in English, but you must place a minimum 50,000-lire order. This shop has the highest recommendation not only for the products, but for Clarissa's care and consideration for all of her customers, whether first-time visitors or long-time regulars.

Giorgio Traversari
Via Guicciardini, 120 (just over Ponte Vecchio)

TELEPHONE 28.77.47

HOURS Winter: Tues–Sat 9 A.M.–1 P.M. and 3:20–7:30 P.M.; summer: Mon–Fri 8:30 A.M.–7:30 P.M.

CREDIT CARDS AMEX, MC, V

TYPE Jewelry

Sterling silver jewelry for reasonable prices. Earrings from $40.

Giulio Giannini & Figlio
Piazza Pitti, 37
TELEPHONE 21.26.21
HOURS Mon–Sat 9 A.M.–7:30 P.M.; closed Mon Mar 15–Nov 15; high season open Sunday
CREDIT CARDS AMEX, MC, V
TYPE Marbleized paper products

The original marbleized paper shop in Florence, started in 1856 and in the same family for five generations. You will see their designs all over Florence, but the ones here are not copies. Everything is done by hand, and is lovely. The prices are higher, but the quality is unsurpassed.

The shop is across the square in front of the Pitti Palace. In this square are rows of hawkers selling everything from fake Louis Vuitton bags to wind-up barking dogs.

Il Torchino
Via dei Bardi, 17
TELEPHONE 234.28.26
HOURS Mon–Sat 9:30 A.M.–1 P.M. and 3:30–7:30 P.M.; closed Mon morning in winter
CREDIT CARDS AMEX, MC, V
TYPE Marbleized paper products

Because everything is made on site, you will find some of the best prices for the Florentine specialty of marbleized paper products at Il Torchino. All the pieces are designed and made here, and you can watch the artists at work. You will find everything from photo frames, albums, diaries, address books, jewelry boxes, and papered pencils. If you do not see a design you like, they will make up sets to order. Fast service.

La Maiolica
Via Guelfa, 31
TELEPHONE 28.00.29
HOURS Winter: Mon 3:30–7:30 P.M., Tues–Sat 9 A.M.–1 P.M. and 3:30–7:30 P.M.; summer: Mon–Fri 9 A.M.–1 P.M. and 3:30–7:30 P.M.; Sat 9 A.M.–1 P.M.
CREDIT CARDS AMEX, DC, MC, V
TYPE Ceramics

One of the nicest and most interesting ceramic shops in Florence. You can watch dishes being made in the main room, which also has the kiln and the displays. The artist will make things to order and have them shipped to your home. Excellent quality and wonderful service; top recommendation. *Note:* All pieces are lead free and dishwasher safe.

Madova Gloves
Factory Piazza S. Felicita, 4; shop Via Guicciardini, 1
TELEPHONE 239.65.26
HOURS 9:30 A.M.–7:30 P.M. daily
CREDIT CARDS MC, V
TYPE Gloves
This shop sells only gloves made in its own factory. They can make a pair of gloves from the tracing of a hand, or make gloves for hands difficult to fit. The gloves come in every type of leather and color, and may be lined in cashmere, silk, or wool. Free shipping.

Officina Profumo Farmaceutica di Santa Maria Novella
Via della Scala, 16
TELEPHONE 21.62.76
HOURS Tues–Sat 8:30 A.M.–12:30 P.M. and 3–7 P.M.
CREDIT CARDS AMEX, MC, V
TYPE Herbal preparations
This is *not* a pharmacy, but an *erboristeria*, a shop selling herbal remedies in what was once the chapel of a Renaissance monastery. It is worth a visit if only to view the spectacular frescoed vaulted ceilings. The Dominican monks who once ran the pharmacy have gone, but you can still buy their medicinal liqueurs or Catherine Deneuve's favorite face cream. Also there is pomegranate soap, honey, lotions, and natural beauty products.

Sezione Aurea
Borgo Ognissanti, 136; telephone: 28.72.70
Via dei Servi, 46; telephone: 239.61.43
Lungarno Acciaioli, 3; telephone: 21.02.33
Via Capo le Case, 20; telephone, 679.27.56
HOURS Winter: Tues–Sat 9:30 A.M.–1 P.M. and 3:30–7:30 P.M.; summer: Mon 4–8 P.M., Tues–Sat 9:30 A.M.–1 P.M. and 4–8 P.M., Sun 10 A.M.–2 P.M.
CREDIT CARDS AMEX, MC, V
TYPE Jewelry
A beautiful selection of handmade acrylic jewelry at reasonable prices. These are one-of-a-kind items you will never see elsewhere.

Standa
Via de' Panzani, 31
TELEPHONE 28.30.71
HOURS 9 A.M.–7:30 P.M., Mon 2–7:30 P.M.
CREDIT CARDS MC, V
TYPE Dry goods and more
The K-Mart of Italy, Standa sells housewares, clothing, and cosmetics.

Sugar Blues Health Food Store
Via XXVII Aprile, 46–48; telephone: 48.36.66
Via dei Serragli, 57; telephone: 26.83.78

HOURS Mon–Tues and Thurs 9:30 A.M.–1:30 P.M. and 4–8 P.M.; closed Wed afternoon

CREDIT CARDS None

TYPE Health foods

A very good health food store selling vitamins, packaged foods, a small selection of deli items, cereals, juices, macrobiotic foods, teas, honeys, yogurt, and cosmetics. If you are hungry for your favorite healthy cereal, chances are they have it, or something very similar.

TAF
Via Por S. Maria, 17

TELEPHONE 239.60.37

HOURS Mon 3:30–7:30 P.M., Tues–Sat 9:30 A.M.–1 P.M. and 3:30–7:30 P.M.

CREDIT CARDS AMEX, DC, MC, V

TYPE Linens and clothing

Exceptional table linens, towels, and sheets in one store, and across the street, household linens, children's clothes, women's blouses, christening gowns, and more. Many things are handmade.

The Gold Corner
Piazza Santa Croce, 15

TELEPHONE 24.19.71

HOURS April–Sept: daily 9:30 A.M.–7 P.M., Oct–Mar: Mon 3–6 P.M., Tues–Sat 9:30 A.M.–1 P.M. and 3–6:30 P.M.; closed Jan

CREDIT CARDS AMEX, DC, MC, V

TYPE Jewelry

Gold sold by weight. It works out to be a *little* less expensive. The selection is huge, and you can certainly find something in your price range. Also, Raymond Weil and Fendi watches and cameos at 20 percent off if you pay in cash, and 15 percent off if you pay by credit card. Ask for the owner, Rosy Miranda Bordo.

The Leather School
Inside the monastery of Santa Croce, entrance through church at Piazza S. Croce, 16, or through garden on Via S. Giuseppe, 5

TELEPHONE 24.45.33

HOURS Tues–Sat 9 A.M.–12:30 P.M. and 3–6 P.M., Easter–Oct open daily

CREDIT CARDS AMEX, MC, V
TYPE Leather goods
This tends to be touristy, but the prices are good. Be sure to look over the items carefully. The selection is very good.

Tre Art
Borgo Ognissanti, 88
TELEPHONE 239.67.53
HOURS Mon 3–7 P.M., Tues–Sat 10 A.M.–1 P.M. and 2–7 P.M.
CREDIT CARDS AMEX, DC, MC, V
TYPE Ceramics
Factory outlet shop for hand-painted Italian ceramic dishes. All are dishwasher safe. Beautiful displays to inspire you. They ship.

Upim
Via Speziali, 3
TELEPHONE None
HOURS Summer: Mon–Sat 9 A.M.–8 P.M.; winter: Mon 2–7:30 P.M., Tues–Sat 9 A.M.–7:30 P.M.
CREDIT CARDS MC, V
TYPE Department store
A national chain of department stores, with a complete range of clothes, cosmetics, and housewares at middle-of-the-road prices.

Vetrina
Borgo degli Albizi, 23
TELEPHONE 24.45.38
HOURS Mon 4–7:30 P.M., Tues–Sat 10 A.M.–1 P.M. and 4–7:30 P.M.
CREDIT CARDS AMEX, MC, V
TYPE Jewelry
Plexiglass jewelry for those who dare to be different. Rings starting at 12,000 lire make great tuck-in gifts for the fans back home.

MARKETS IN FLORENCE
Esselunga Supermarket
Via Pisana, 130, and Viale de Amicis, 89 (not close to central Florence)
HOURS Mon–Tues and Thurs–Sat 9 A.M.–7 P.M. and Wed 9 A.M.–1 P.M.
CREDIT CARDS No
This is the best American-style supermarket in Florence. Avoid Saturdays and late afternoons after 5 o'clock. The best time to go is in the morning and during the lunch hour. Lots of free parking.

Mercato di San Lorenzo (Central Market in Florence)
Piazza del Mercato Centrale, next to San Lorenzo church
TELEPHONE None
HOURS Mon–Sat 7 A.M.–1 P.M., Sat afternoon 4–7:30 P.M.
CREDIT CARDS No

Three floors of food sold in individual stalls. A real experience. On the ground floor are animals and fish, and upstairs are fruit and vegetables. There are also places to have a cappuccino with the sellers, as well as stalls selling bread, wines, and household items. Around the outside, hundreds of stalls sell leather, Florentine paper goods, scarves, umbrellas, bags, T-shirts—you name it. The prices are sometimes negotiable. Always watch for quality and honesty. Stand No. 4 has fake Gucci scarves. This entire experience is well worth a few hours; plan to have lunch somewhere around the market (see *Cheap Eats in Italy* for suggestions).

Mercato Nuovo (Straw Market)
Logge del Mercato Nuovo, Via Por Santa Maria
TELEPHONE None
HOURS Daily 9 A.M.–5 P.M.
CREDIT CARDS Depends on individual stall, but usually yes
TYPE Straw and tourist-oriented goods

Although you can find some straw products (hats, place mats), most stalls sell linens, leather, fake designer bags, jewelry, and tourist kitsch. Worth a stroll through.

SHOPPING STREETS
Borgo dei Greci

This street is loaded with one leather shop after another, selling everything from tiny boxes to handbags, shoes, and coats. There is lots of junk, so be sure to look at several stores before you decide to purchase. One of the best shops on this street is Peruzzi, at No. 12. Across the street, look at Botega Fiorentina. Don't forget the leather school in the Santa Croce Monastery at the end of the street (see page 168).

Lungarno Accaiaioli, 22

This street runs along the Arno River from Piazza Goldoni to the Ponte Vecchio and is filled with one shop after another. All are lovely and most are expensive, but the street is well worth time spent browsing and checking inside if something appeals to you.

Via Tornabuoni
The premier shopping street in Florence, with all the big-name designers. Side streets worth a stroll are Via delle Vigna Nuova, Via delle Spade, and Via delle Sole.

SHOPPING IN ROME

SHOPPING HOURS
October–June: Mon 3:30–7:30 P.M., Tues–Sat 9 A.M.–1 P.M. and 3:30–7:30 P.M.

June–Sept: Mon–Fri 9 A.M.–1 P.M. and 4–8 P.M., Sat 9 A.M.–1 P.M.

Food shops 8:30 A.M.–1 P.M. and 5–7:30 P.M. year around

Rome is not the shopper's paradise that Milan, Florence, and Venice are. Oh yes, there are beautiful shops, but prices are high unless you are lucky enough to be there during the twice-yearly sales. For the best buys, look for leather, knits, jewelry, and shoes. If you want religious items blessed by the Pope, head for Via Conciliazone, which leads to St. Peter's Square, and you will find everything you want in every price range.

An occasional visitor to Rome never makes it to the Vatican at all, but no one misses the Piazza di Spagna (Spanish Steps). This is the heart of shopping Rome, where the deluxe boutiques of big-name designers beckon crowds of window shoppers admiring the magnificent displays of everything from fashion to home furnishings. Just two blocks from these famous shops along Via Condotti is Via Frattina, where you will find high-quality merchandise, but at *slightly* lower prices. Cheap Chic shoppers will love the authentic neighborhoods around Campo de' Fiori and Piazza Navona, and the winding, narrow streets of Trastevere. Less expensive shops are also across the Tiber on Via Cola di Rienzo and Via Ottaviano. And don't forget the earthy open-air markets as great places to find something reasonably priced.

American Book Shop
Via della Vite, 27 & 57
TELEPHONE 679.52.22
HOURS Mon 4–8 P.M., Tues–Sat 9 A.M.–1 P.M. and 3:30–7:30 P.M.; closed Aug
CREDIT CARDS AMEX, DC, MC, V
TYPE Bookshop

A tiny English-language bookshop loaded with everything you will need: guidebooks, art history and architecture, paperback fiction. Prices are higher than in the United States, but if you need a book, this is the place.

Ancora Book Shop
Via della Conciliazione, 63
TELEPHONE 656.88.20
HOURS Mon–Fri, 9 A.M.–1 P.M. and 3:30–7:30 P.M., Sat 9 A.M.–1 P.M.
CREDIT CARDS AMEX, DC, MC, V
TYPE Bookshop
A Catholic bookshop. Look upstairs for English-language titles. They have a selection of guides on Rome.

Anticoli
Piazza Mignanelli, 21 (near American Express office on Piazza di Spagna)
TELEPHONE 678.44.96
HOURS Mon 3–7 P.M., Tues–Sat 9:30 A.M.–1:30 P.M. and 3–7 P.M.
CREDIT CARDS AMEX, MC, V
TYPE Leather accessories
Gloves, wallets, and purses sold from bins. Also better-quality gloves, belts, and so on at factory prices. This shop has been in the same family for three generations.

Balloon
Piazza di Spagna, 35 (look for green doors at rear courtyard on left side of American Express office)
TELEPHONE 578.01.10
HOURS Mon–Sat 10:30 A.M.–9:30 P.M.
CREDIT CARDS AMEX, DC, MC, V
TYPE Clothing
This chain has many outlets in Italy, including nine in Rome. They have good prices on tailored clothes for men and women. The selection is enormous. Many items are from China, so look carefully for faulty workmanship. Good for the yuppie dresser.

Da Roma
Via delle Muratte, 96
TELEPHONE 678.09.38
HOURS Winter: Tues–Sat 9 A.M.–8 P.M.; summer: Mon–Sat 9 A.M.–8 P.M.
CREDIT CARDS AMEX, DC, MC, V

TYPE Clothing

Exclusive designs for T-shirts, silk ties, sweaters, jogging outfits. *Way* above average, with realistic prices. The best T-shirts in Rome, and not touristy.

Discount System
Via Viminale, 35
TELEPHONE 47.46.545

HOURS Mon 3:30–7:30 P.M., Tues–Sat 9 A.M.–1 P.M. and 3:30–7:30 P.M.

CREDIT CARDS No

TYPE Clothing and more

Fifty percent off on all designer clothes, luggage, belts, bags, umbrellas. They have dressing rooms with mirrors. The best discount game in town. Clothes for men and women.

Economy Book Center
Via Torino, 136
TELEPHONE 474.68.77

HOURS Mon 3–7:30 P.M., Tues–Fri 9:30 A.M.–7:30 P.M., Sat 9:30 A.M.–3 P.M.

CREDIT CARDS AMEX, DC, MC, V

TYPE Bookshop

Paul Goldfield runs a great bookshop. He will buy or give store credit for your used English-language books. He also stocks a good selection of magazines, cards, books for children, videotapes, books on tape, and travel books.

G. B. Panatta Fine Arts Shop
Via Francesco Crispi, 117
TELEPHONE 679.59.48

HOURS Mon 3:30–7:30 P.M., Tues–Sat 10 A.M.–1 P.M. and 3:30–7:30 P.M.

CREDIT CARDS No

TYPE Paper art goods

A good selection of nice art cards and postcards, attractive prints, some nice Florentine paper, and painted boxes. Well priced.

Il Discount Dell'Alta Mode
Via Gesùe Maria, 16A
TELEPHONE Not available

HOURS Mon 3:30–7:30 P.M., Tues–Sat 9:30 A.M.–1 P.M. and 3:30–7:30 P.M.

CREDIT CARDS No

TYPE Designer clothing

Overstocks of designer labels such as Giorgio Armani, Jean-Paul Gaultier, and Claude Montana. About 50 percent off. A limited supply of handbags, umbrellas, and accessories. No defective merchandise. Very good, but selection varies. You may hit pay dirt one day and strike out the next four or five visits. Well worth checking if you are a dedicated Cheap Chic shopper.

La Rinascente
Via del Corso at corner of Piazza Colonna

TELEPHONE 679.76.91

HOURS Mon 3:30–7:30 P.M., Tues–Sat 9:30 A.M.–7:30 P.M.

CREDIT CARDS AMEX, DC, MC, V

TYPE Department store

Foreign visitors can ask for the Hostess Tourist Service and get a hostess-interpreter as a guide to all departments. By American standards, this is a very small department store, but they do offer one-stop shopping. They give a discount on cosmetics and the *detasse* (export tax) refund, but you have to spend over $600 right there to get it.

Leone Cimentari
Via Portico d'Ottavia, 47

TELEPHONE 654.06.89

CREDIT CARDS V

TYPE China and kitchenware

A discounted china store selling almost every pattern known. Not for the delicate shopper. This place is big, dirty, and dusty, and you must do a lot of shopping on your own. Bring gloves and a rag. They will ship. Prices are about 20 percent off regular retail. In addition to china, look for kitchenware, crystal, silver, and pots and pans. Plan on one hour just to case the place, then go back and make your selection. A good place to fill in your own china pattern. It is worth the trip and the long waits at the checkout counter. When ready to buy, ask for an English-speaking clerk.

Mas
Piazza Vittorio Emanuele

TELEPHONE None available

HOURS Mon 3:30–7:30 P.M., Tues–Sat 9 A.M.–1 P.M. and 3:30–7:30 P.M.

CREDIT CARDS AMEX, MC, V

TYPE Bargains

If you love Pic-n-Save, Tati in Paris, or Filene's bargain basement, you are a candidate for Mas. There are mounds of clothes, shoes, suitcases, sundries, umbrellas, hats, scarves, sweaters (even cashmere!), bedding (Bassetti), and more, at prices you won't believe. Across the street is a fur and leather division. If you approach on Via Carlo Libero, you will pass one jewelry and hair ornament shop after another, all cheap. This shopping experience takes time and endurance and is recommended *only* for the hardcore Cheap Chic shopper. There are dressing rooms and clerks and fashions for everyone in the family. In the square across the street is a huge outdoor market, but watch out for the Gypsies who swarm in around 12:30 as it is about to close. The clothes here are awful, but the foodstuffs are typically displayed and it all adds up to an interesting hour of wandering through (see Piazza Vittorio Emanuele, page 176).

Pappagallo
Via Francesco Crispi, 115A
TELEPHONE 678.30.11
HOURS Mon 3:30–7:30 P.M., Tues–Sat 9 A.M.–1 P.M. and 3:30–7:30 P.M.
CREDIT CARDS AMEX, DC, MC, V
TYPE Factory prices for suede and leather
Decent prices; not in the giveaway range, but fair. Good sales, with up to 50 percent off.

Standa
Viale Trastevere
TELEPHONE None
HOURS Mon 2–7:30 P.M., Tues–Sat 9 A.M.–7:30 P.M.
CREDIT CARDS MC, V
TYPE Food and department store
A supermarket and a dimestore-quality department store. Good if you need a few quick things. The prices are the best in Rome.

The Corner Bookshop
Via del Moro, 48
TELEPHONE 583.69.42
HOURS Mon 3:30–7:30 P.M., Tues–Sat 9:30 A.M.–1 P.M. and 3:30–7:30 P.M.
CREDIT CARDS MC, V
TYPE Bookshop
English-language books exclusively. Owned by Claire Hammond, who is delightful and knowledgeable. She can order for you. A nice Trastevere location.

Upim
Via del Tritone, 172
TELEPHONE None
HOURS Mon 3:30–7:30 P.M., Tues–Sat 9 A.M.–1 P.M. and 3:30–7:30 P.M.
CREDIT CARDS MC, V
TYPE Department store
This is really a high-class dimestore, but it is great fun for the cosmetics of the moment, a bottle of hand lotion, or a practical piece of clothing.

ROME MARKETS, FLEA AND OTHERWISE
Piazza Fontanella Borghese—Antiques Market
HOURS Mon–Sat 9 A.M.–6 P.M.
CREDIT CARDS Depends on individual stall
This is a small market at the end of the square. It has permanent stalls selling prints, stamps, old postcards and books, some jewelry, and assorted knickknacks. The prices tend to be high, but there may be something that will catch your eye. It pays to bargain.

Mercato di Porta Portese — Flea Market
Along the Tiber; best entrance at Viale Trastevere. Take bus No. 75 to Porta di Portese, then walk to Via Portuense
HOURS Sunday only, 6 A.M.–2 P.M.
CREDIT CARDS Best to use cash
Over 1,000 sellers offering everything you can imagine: some fake, some hot, and some not. If you like this sort of thing, don't miss it.

Piazza Vittorio Emanuele — Outdoor Market
HOURS Mon–Sat 7 A.M.–2 P.M.
A covered outdoor market with everything you ever needed, or thought you might. You will find live chickens, rabbits, clothing, jeans, flowers, meats, cheeses, and produce—all at good prices. Watch out for pickpockets, especially when the stalls start shutting down about 1:15 and the Gypsy crowds arrive to do their daily marketing. Be careful; these people are pros!

Via dell'Arancio (near the end of Via Ripetta)—Outdoor Morning Produce and Flower Market
HOURS Mon–Sat 8 A.M.–1 P.M.
This small market in a high-end neighborhood makes up in quality what it lacks in size. If you keep going back to the same stall, after four or five visits you will be treated like a regular.

SHOPPING STREETS

The following streets are lined with beautiful shops and are well worth a stroll. You won't be alone in your strolling, especially late in the afternoon or on Sunday, when it seems as though all of Rome is out browsing and window shopping. Most of the things in these stores are expensive, but now and then you will find a bargain, especially during the January sales.

Via Borgogna	Chic and expensive shops with beautiful displays.
Via Cola di Rienzo	Be sure to see Castinori at No. 99, a huge gourmet grocery store. This street has modestly priced shops, including Standa, the lowest-priced supermarket in Rome.
Via Condotti	Probably the most famous shopping street in Rome.
Via dei Gambero	Boutiques.
Via della Croce	Luscious food shops.
Via del Babuino	Designers.
Via Frattina	More famous and near-famous designers.
Via Margutta	Art galleries and antiques.

SHOPPING IN VENICE

SHOPPING HOURS
Winter: Mon 3:30–7:30 P.M., Tues–Fri 9 A.M.–1 P.M. and 3:30–7:30 P.M., Sat 9 A.M.–1 P.M.

Summer: Mon–Tues 9 A.M.–1 P.M. and 3:30–7:30 P.M., Sat 9 A.M.–1 P.M.

Beginning with Marco Polo, the Venetians controlled trade with the East, bringing silks and spices to the European continent. The trading spirit continues to this day, as millions of visitors flock to the city not only to enjoy its unique beauty and art, but to purchase handmade lace, beautiful glassware, colorful fabrics, and pâpiér-mache Carnevale masks. Most shopkeepers speak English, and are used to tourists and anxious for their business.

The maze of winding streets crisscrossed by canals and bridges will prove frustrating for the shopper with limited time. Please do not worry about getting lost; everyone does, and it is part of the charm and adventure of Venice. Besides, who knows? You may discover some wonderful restaurant, the perfect hotel, or a hidden shop you otherwise would have missed.

Capricci e Vanità
San Pantalon, 3744

AREA Dorsoduro

TELEPHONE 523.15.04

HOURS Mon 4–7 P.M., Tues–Fri 9:30 A.M.–1 P.M. and 4–7:30 P.M., Sat 9:30 A.M.–1 P.M.

CREDIT CARDS AMEX, MC, V

TYPE Antique lace and clothing

This is a charming one-of-a-kind shop specializing in antique lace, dresses from the forties, fifties, and sixties, and hats.

Coin Department Store
Salizzada San Giovanni Crisotomo, 5788

AREA Cannaregio

TELEPHONE 52.27.192

HOURS Mon 3–7 P.M., Tues–Sat 9:30 A.M.–1 P.M. and 3–7:30 P.M.

CREDIT CARDS MC, V

Four floors of clothing for the whole family. This chain store is based in Milan and also sells reasonably priced (for Italy) cosmetics and perfumes. There is also a small houseware section.

Dimodí
Campo S. Filippo e Giancomo, 4523

AREA Castello

TELEPHONE 523.51.87

HOURS Winter: Mon 3–7:30 P.M., Tues–Sat 9:30 A.M.–1 P.M. and 3–7:30 P.M.; summer: 9:30 A.M.–8 P.M. daily

CREDIT CARDS AMEX, DC, MC, V

TYPE Gifts

A good selection of unusual silk scarves, costume jewelry, gloves, and umbrellas.

FM Art Shop—Il Prato
Frezzeria, 1771

AREA San Marco

TELEPHONE 520.70.45

HOURS Winter: Mon 2–7:30 P.M., Tues–Sat 10:30 A.M.–1 P.M. and 2–7:30 P.M.; summer: open Sunday

CREDIT CARDS AMEX, DC, MC, V
TYPE Watercolors and etchings by Franco Mazzucchi

Franco Mazzucchi sells his own watercolors and etchings of Venice at very fair prices. He is a real artist, not the touristy type one sees in other parts of Venice. Other artists are also represented. You can buy an original watercolor with a nice frame for under $100, and when you consider the cost of framing alone in the States, this is a good price.

Il Coccio di Marina
Salizzada dei Greci, 3446
AREA Castello
TELEPHONE 528.58.84
HOURS Mon 3:30–7:30 P.M., Tues–Sat 10 A.M.–1:30 P.M. and 3:30–7:30 P.M.; closed Aug
CREDIT CARDS MC, V
TYPE Antique beads

Marina Scarpa uses all her own designs in creating unusual jewelry made from antique Venetian glass beads. She will make things to order, and you can call for an appointment. She and her husband paint the masks that hang on the walls.

Island of Murano
Murano
TYPE Glass making

Though Venice's major glass makers have shops around San Marco, it is much more interesting to go directly to the source on Murano. Prices are competitive. Try to negotiate on large purchases, not souvenirs. Do not fall for the many hawkers touting "a free trip to Murano." These men prowl the wharf along the Grand Canal and the streets leading to it with offers of free boat trips to the island. Once you are on one of these boats, you are obliged to go to the shops they represent and they get a commission for sending you. These shops do not have low prices. Better to spend a few lire and take the boat at Stop No. 5 along the Grand Canal, or No. 12 from Fondamente Nuove.

Liberia Emiliana
Calle Goldoni, 4487
AREA San Marco
TELEPHONE 522.07.93
HOURS Winter: Mon 3–7:30 P.M., Tues–Sat 9 A.M.–12:30 P.M. and 3–7:30 P.M.; summer: Mon–Sat 9–7:30 P.M.
CREDIT CARDS AMEX, DC, MC, V

TYPE Bookstore with English-language titles

Here you can purchase English-language novels, cookbooks, travel books (Michelin Guides), books about Italy, histories of Venice, maps, and a large selection of paperback books on aviation.

Mercatino dell'Antiquariato
Campo S. Maurizio
TELEPHONE None

CREDIT CARDS Depends on stall seller

TYPE Antiques market

There are no hidden bargains, but this yearly antiques market held during Easter is worth at least a pass-through to see if something catches your eye. There are prints, old jewelry (be careful; some of it falls apart), and tidbits that are easy to tuck into a corner of your suitcase.

For the exact dates, contact Aziendadi Promozione Turistica, Piazza San Marco, 71C, Ascensione 522.63.56.

Rigattieri
At Campo Sant'Angelo and Campo San Stefano, Campiello San Stefano, 3532–36
AREA San Marco

TELEPHONE 523.10.81

HOURS Mon 3–7:30 P.M., Tues–Sat 9 A.M.–1 P.M. and 3–7:30 P.M.

CREDIT CARDS AMEX, DC, MC, V

TYPE Ceramics

One of the widest selections of Italian ceramics in Venice. They will ship.

Scuola dei Merletti
Piazza B. Galuppi
AREA Burano

TELEPHONE 73.00.34

HOURS Mon, Wed–Fri 9 A.M.–6 P.M.

CREDIT CARDS No

TYPE Handmade lace

MISCELLANEOUS How to get to Burano: Take the Line No. 12 vaporetto, which also goes to Murano (the glass-making island). Boats leave from the Fondamente Nuove every hour.

The island of Burano has been famous for centuries for its lace making. The lace-making school began in 1872. Today they are open to the public, selling goods from their beautiful modern and traditional collection of table and bed linens. There is also a museum, which displays magnificent pieces of old lace. While the prices at the school are not bargains, they are fair. There are many shops selling lace on Burano. The best advice is to browse first and then go back and buy, all the time trying not to become too confused by the seemingly unlimited selection.

Veneziartigiana
Calle larga San Marco, 412–13
AREA San Marco
TELEPHONE 523.50.32
HOURS Mon 3:30–8 P.M., Tues–Sat 10 A.M.–8 P.M.
CREDIT CARDS MC, V
TYPE A collection of Venetian specialties made by local artists
This is a good one-stop shopping experience if you are pressed for time, yet still want to take home some quality Venetian crafts. Here local artists display their work, ranging from glass and paper to linens and lace. Prices are reasonable.

OUTDOOR MARKETS
Campo S. Barnaba Dorsoduro
A floating market where you can buy off the boats. Open Mon–Tues and Thurs–Sat 9 A.M.–1 P.M. and 3:30–7:30 P.M., Wed 9 A.M.–1 P.M.

Campo S. Margherita, Dorsoduro
A few stalls with fruits, vegetables, and fish. The best time is Saturday morning. Open Mon, Tues, and Thurs–Sat 9 A.M.–1 P.M. and 3:30–7:30 P.M.

Rialto Markets
The market stalls lining the bridge sell everything from T-shirts and glassware to fake and real lace. Worth a stroll for take-home souvenirs, but bargains are rare. Vegetable market Mon–Sat 8 A.M.–1 P.M.; fish market Tues–Sat 8 A.M.–1 P.M.
The vegetable (*erberia*) and fish (*pescheria*) markets are the best, least expensive, and most colorful in Venice. The vegetable market sells anything that cannot be bought in the fish market. It has stalls loaded with seasonal fruits, vegetables, cheeses, wine, and meats. Definitely worth a trip, and you should bring your camera.
The fish market is thought by many to be the finest in Europe. Here you will see every known variety of fresh fish, and some you never knew existed. Again, this is worth a trip, and don't forget your camera.

INDEXES

FLORENCE INDEX

Geographical Index

Big Splurges

Other Options

ROME INDEX

Geographical Index

Big Splurges

Other Options

VENICE INDEX

Geographical Index

Big Splurges

Other Options

SHOPPING INDEX

READERS' COMMENTS

While every effort has been made to provide accurate information in this guide, the publisher and author cannot be held responsible for changes in any of the listings due to rate increases, inflation, dollar fluctuation, the passage of time, or changes in management.

Cheap Sleeps in Italy is updated and revised on a regular basis. If you find a change before I do, or make an important discovery you want to pass along to me, please send a note stating the name and address of the hotel or shop, the date of your visit, and a description of your findings. Your comments are very important. I investigate every complaint and hand out every compliment you send me about your favorite hotel or shop.

Send your comments to Sandra A. Gustafson (*Cheap Sleeps in Italy*), c/o Chronicle Books, 275 Fifth Street, San Francisco, CA 94103.

Other titles in the *Cheap Eats* and *Cheap Sleeps* travel series by Sandra A. Gustafson:

Cheap Eats in Paris
Cheap Sleeps in Paris
Cheap Eats in London
Cheap Sleeps in London

These and additional Chronicle Books titles are available at your local bookstore. For a color catalog of all our books, call or write:

Chronicle Books
275 Fifth Street
San Francisco, California 94103
1-800-722-6657